MISSION POSSIBLE
AN INVESTMENT GUIDE FOR CHRISTIANS

MISSION POSSIBLE
AN INVESTMENT GUIDE FOR CHRISTIANS

STEPHEN H. HAMMOND

Unless otherwise indicated, Scripture quotations are taken from the King James Version of the Bible.

Scripture quotations marked *NKJV* are from the *New King James Version*. Copyright © 1979, 1980, 1982, 1990, 1995, Thomas Nelson Inc., Publishers.

Stock charts courtesy of Telescan.

Book Editor: Wanda Griffith
Editorial Assistant: Tammy Hatfield
Copy Editors: Esther Metaxas
Cresta Shawver
Oreeda Burnette
Inside Layout: Mark Shuler

Library of Congress Catalog Card Number: 2002108313
ISBN: 0-87148-621-0
Copyright © 2002 by Pathway Press
Cleveland, Tennessee 37311
All Rights Reserved
Printed in the United States of America

DEDICATION

To my wife,
Angela,
my son,
David,
and my daughter,
Rachel.

Also to my parents, who were beacons of light
that showed me the way less traveled.

To my sister,
Shanda,
and brother,
Timothy,
along with Christian friends who
helped make this book become a reality through their prayers.

A special remembrance goes to my grandfather
Jesse Matthew Aycock
(1911-1993).

Contents

    Foreword 9

    Introduction 11

1. A Christian Path to Wealth 15
2. Avenues to God's Blessings 19
3. Budgeting and Savings 31
4. Investing and Accumulating Wealth 47
5. The Selection Process 61
6. Asset Allocation and Diversification 71
7. Stock Section/Fundamental Analysis 85
8. Technical Analysis/Reading Charts 99
9. When to Sell 127
10. Do Not Lose Focus 137
    Appendix 141

Foreword

Money is an inescapable aspect of life. Throughout the centuries, wealth has been measured by livestock, land, salt, gold and currency. Men die seeking riches; wars are always fought for economic reasons. For the Christian, there is nothing wrong with being successful. However, we must be good stewards of our money, since it is provided by God and not without incumbent responsibility.

It has been said that for every man with a dollar, there are several men trying to take it away from him. This practical, straightforward book will show the reader how to not only hold on to those dollars, but also how to make them grow in good times and bad. There is no mysterious secret revealed within, just a systematic, disciplined approach that will enable the reader to gain and maintain wealth over a lifetime.

This approach requires wisdom, practice and commitment in order to succeed. The Book of James tells us that if we lack wisdom, we may ask God, who will grant us wisdom. We must then put that wisdom into practice to achieve the goal of wealth accumulation and preservation to which we are committed. Stephen Hammond demonstrates how to accomplish this task in his easy-to-read book. The author is a seasoned asset manager and financial advisor with nearly two decades of experience. He is an unwavering Christian. His book is based solidly on Biblical principles of financial acumen. In fact, the reader will notice Scripture references on nearly every page. This is comforting, for Christians know that the Bible is the only infallible rule of faith and practice. Stephen Hammond once told me that he could make money for me from my investment. Read this book and let him show you how to do the same.

Jack R. Eades, MD
Southern Allergy & Asthma, PC

INTRODUCTION

This book is written for Christians who are being misinformed about how and why to accumulate wealth and invest their hard-earned money. The Christian media and pulpits across America tell us that God wants to bless us, but they say little about how the child of God can open up avenues through which God can pour out His blessings, including financial blessings.

Instead, many pastors in churches and on TV teach that God is going to rain blessings out of heaven the way He rained manna down for the children of Israel as they wandered through the desert. As believers, we are not going to wake up one morning and find money standing like dew in our backyards. Rather, God will bless those who have been faithful to His Word. In simple language, God's blessings come through the ordinary world: healthy bodies, vibrant minds and material wealth.

Few of us are foolish enough to believe God will bless with exceptional health those who eat poorly, never exercise and abuse their bodies with nicotine, alcohol and drugs. While we believe God wants to bless His children with fine health, we also recognize that we can undermine those blessings with unhealthy habits. Why, then, do we believe God will send financial blessings to His children who fail to exercise their financial muscles any more than they exercise their physical muscles? Why do we think God will bless those who burden their financial body with excessive debt the same way they burden their physical body with excessive fat? God wants His children to be both healthy and wealthy, and He is ready to pour out blessings, both wealth and health, to those who keep His Word and exercise that Word. If you live a slack life, then you should not expect either health or wealth, even though God wants you to have both. If you want the blessings of God, then you must get up from your spiritual, physical and financial sofa and exercise the mind, body and spirit God gave you.

This book teaches how God blesses His children through the actions and efforts of people, and that financial success is one of His primary blessings. This book, then, will provide the Christian believer with specific, time-tested instructions for moving from an impoverished and weak lifestyle to a wealthy and healthy lifestyle. It will also show you how to create avenues through which God can bestow His financial blessings. The mission is not easy, but it is possible. As the Bible teaches us, "All things are possible for those who believe" (see Mark 9:23).

Some Christians may challenge the idea that we should strive for wealth in the same way we might strive for health. However, we must remember that the Lord our God gives us the power to get wealth (see Deuteronomy 8:18). All good things are from God, but is wealth good?

Like health, wealth in itself is not sinful. Wealth does not constitute sin until it is used contrary to God's Word. For example, if we use our good health simply to satisfy the desires of the flesh, as many people do, our health is no blessing from God and blesses neither others nor us. We would have been better off without good health. Jesus said, "If your eye offends, then pluck it out, for better to be blind than to lose your soul" (see Matthew 5:29;18:9). Likewise, if we use our wealth to satisfy our evil impulses, then that wealth is no blessing from God, and it does not bless others. If our wealth only satisfies ourselves and brings offense to our neighbors and to God, we would be better off poor.

Both health and wealth, then, can be a stumbling block to individuals who pursue a life of evil. The Bible clearly warns us of this danger. However, it is wrong to suggest that the Bible teaches that the pursuit of either health or wealth is evil. Rather, the Bible shows us that the blessings of God can be subverted if we are not diligent to keep His commandments. Evil delights in taking one of God's blessings and turning it into something foul, wrong and bad.

Wealth, then, is not evil in itself. Rather, it is one of God's blessings for His people, just like good health. However, this is not the entire story. It isn't just OK for Christians to pursue wealth—it is our duty, just as it is our duty to pursue good health. How is this so? Read on. I trust that you will be receptive to the principles outlined in God's Word.

A Christian Path to Wealth

God has given each of us a marvelous body, and He expects us not to abuse it with habits, lifestyles and substances that pollute and damage His temple (see 1 Corinthians 3:16). God's Word promises rich blessings if we take care of our bodies.

Each of you reading this book has a source of income: a salary, a wage, a pension, some collection of money God has placed in your care and through which He wants to bless you and those around you. As with our bodies, God expects us to make the most of our resources. Just like with our bodies, the Bible clearly opposes habits, lifestyles and substances that damage our wealth and prevent it from growing and being all it can be. It seems so easy for us to accept that God wants us to be healthy. Why do we resist the idea that God also wants us to be wealthy?

Why Accommodate Wealth?

Perhaps the main reason God wants us to be both healthy and wealthy is that He has much work for us to do, and the healthier and wealthier we are, the more work we can do for others and for His kingdom.

Mission Possible

First, we are to care for those who depend on us—our children, parents and families. Then, we are to care for those in our communities, our neighbors who have fallen on hard times. God expects us to make every effort to support those around us who are weaker and less fortunate. His Word commands us to preach the gospel to all the world: "Go ye into all the world, and preach the gospel to every creature" (Mark 16:15).

To do this requires money and wealth, among other things. The more wealth we have, the more we can be one of those avenues God can use. The gospel is free, but it takes health and wealth to send missionaries around the world. It costs money to send preachers into our ghettos and backyards. The Bible tells us, "The laborer is worthy of his hire" (Luke 10:7). These men and women of God are worthy to receive blessing and honor and what financial support we can give them.

When we bless the man or woman of God with some of our financial wealth, we also open avenues for our own blessings. The Shunammite woman is a good example. She blessed Elisha by building a room for him to stay in her house and by providing the very best that she could for him. Even though she was past her childbearing years, God rewarded her deed by giving her a son. Later, when her son died, Elisha prayed and the boy was raised from the dead (see 2 Kings 4:8-35). We cannot outgive God.

Our desire, then, should be to accumulate wealth to establish the kingdom of God, to support the poor and to bless the servants of God. If all Christians were poor, who would help establish God's kingdom? Who would pay for the satellites to send the message of our Lord across the world? It is God's will to bless His people financially and otherwise, and thereby bring blessings to the rest of the world. Our heavenly Father owns the cattle on a thousand hills and the beasts of the forest (Psalm 50:10), and it is His will to bless His children with this wealth. God's Word says if we ask for bread He will not give us a stone. If our earthly fathers know how to give good

A Christian Path to Wealth

gifts, then how much more will our heavenly Father give us good gifts (see Matthew 7:9-11)? He wishes above all things that we would be prosperous, even as our soul prospers (3 John 2). He also tells us that He will give us the desires of our heart (Psalm 37:4).

We should not desire wealth just for personal consumption—"For the love of money is the root of all evil" (1 Timothy 6:10). When we obtain riches from God, we are not to be high-minded by trusting in the wealth we have, but we are to trust in the living God and to distribute tithes and offerings unto the Lord and tell of His good deed toward us (1 Timothy 6:17, 18).

Earlier I said God has provided each of us with marvelous health and wealth. You may have objected, thinking that you are not presently very healthy or wealthy. I did not say God gave us perfect, or optimum, health and wealth. Few of us will be as healthy as an Olympic athlete or as wealthy as Bill Gates. Most of us have both physical and financial limitations from birth, and many of us have added to those limitations through haphazard and careless lifestyles. However, both our bodies and our money can be more than they are now, and they should be more. God expects us to work with and make the most of what He has provided. Any less, and we block the avenues through which God wants to bless us.

The Bible gives an example of some avenues to God's blessings in the account of Job, who was the wealthiest man in the East. God blessed Job financially with sheep, camels, oxen and donkeys. Since livestock was the means to wealth in Job's time, they formed one of the avenues through which God blessed Job. Other avenues of blessing were Job's children, wife, health and social standing. For the sake of this discussion, I will focus on the financial avenues God used to bless Job.

Because our society is not dominated by agriculture and livestock, avenues of financial blessings will include financial instruments such as stocks and mutual funds.

Isn't that marvelous? Donkeys or stocks—it doesn't matter to God. He can use any avenue to bless us with wealth. However, we must keep in mind that we can block almost any avenue to God's blessings through poor habits and lifestyles. We cannot stop God from wanting to bless us, but we can stop Him from doing so. This book is all about how we can unblock the avenues so that God's richest blessings can fill our lives with all He wants for His children.

Avenues to God's Blessings

None of the many financial books in the bookstores today teach you to accumulate wealth by first giving it away. But then, none of those books are written from a Christian perspective, which turns worldly advice upside down. For example, Christ taught that in His kingdom the first would be last, and the last first (Matthew 19:30). This book, then, begins its financial advice with tithing. We must first tithe to be blessed of the Lord.

Tithe

The tithe (tenth) belongs to the Lord. We are to bring all our tithes into the storehouse of God. God tells us in His Word that if we do not pay tithes, we are robbing God (Malachi 3:8). A harsh charge, is it not? Not if we remember that all we have was given to us by God and that all good and perfect gifts come from God (James 1:17). So, if God gives us all we have, should we complain about using 10 percent to further His kingdom?

We must remember that paying tithes is not an option; rather, it is a commandment from God (Leviticus 27:30; Malachi 3:10). I have

Mission Possible

heard some Christians say, "Tithing is not mentioned in the New Testament, so I'm not going to pay my tithes. The old law was done away with, and the new law of Jesus Christ does not mention tithes." These Christians are deceived and are blocking the avenues of God's blessings to themselves and to others.

First of all, God tells us in the Old Testament (the old law) that the tithes are for the priests, or clergy (see Numbers 18:21-24; Nehemiah 10:37) and for God's house (see Malachi 3:10). The Bible further tells us that Jesus (or God) is the same yesterday, today and forever (Hebrews 13:8). In other words, God never changes. Therefore, if God required His children to pay tithes to the clergy and to His house of worship under the old law, then God, under the new law, requires the same of us. God tells us that we are to give offerings into the house of God (Romans 12:13; Philippians 4:15; 1 Timothy 5:17, 18).

Another point to remember is that Jesus Christ is a high priest who is eternal and that the children of Abraham must support the priesthood. You may complain that you are not a child of Abraham, but let me assure you that all born-again Christians are children of Abraham. Abraham, the father of faith, paid tithes to Melchizedek (see Genesis 14:18-20). After the order of Melchizedek (Hebrews 6:20), Jesus Christ was made a high priest. Therefore, as our father of faith, Abraham paid a tenth of all he had to Melchizedek, so we are to pay a tenth of all we have to Christ. And how do we pay tithes to Christ Jesus? By paying tithes to the house of God and to His priests, just as they did in the Old Testament.

God tells us that when we pay our tithes, He will pour out a blessing on us so great that we will not have room enough to receive it (see Luke 6:38). This follows a principle recognized throughout the Bible: If we sow sparingly, we will reap sparingly. If we sow bountifully, we will reap bountifully (2 Corinthians 9:6). We enter God's mainstream of blessings by paying our tithes and offerings unto the Lord.

Avenues of God's Blessings

One of the marvelous privileges of paying tithes is that we can then try, or prove, God. God challenges us to prove Him regarding the rewards of tithing. If we tithe, we will not lack money to carry on God's work. He promises that the windows of heaven will open for the tithe payer, that the devourer (Satan) will be rebuked from the tithe payer, and that men will recognize that the blessing came from God (Malachi 3:10-12). And He challenges us to put His promises to the test.

Personal Experience

My wife, Angela, and I have tested God's promises in our own lives, and we have not been found wanting.

In 1990, I began seeking God's direction in my career as a financial consultant. I was working for a major stock brokerage firm that advocated long-term investing to its clients but paid its financial consultants on a commission basis. This encouraged short-term investing. If a financial consultant did not move money around in his client's portfolio, neither he nor the firm made a good return. In other words, there was a built-in conflict of interest between the financial consultant and his clients.

The clients relied on the financial consultant to do what was best for them (long-term investing), but if the consultant did this, he would not generate enough revenue for the firm and possibly not enough commission to feed his family. There was constant pressure to move money around, a practice the firm referred to as the "velocity of money."

The brokerage firm preached two very different messages. On the inside, they preached high velocity of money, but on the outside, through the media and TV, they preached long-term investing.

I was troubled by this duplicity, believing that I was not truly meeting the financial needs of my clients. Finally, by early 1993, I received the peace and the assurance that it was God's will for me to

Mission Possible

leave my position as a financial consultant and start my own "fee-only" investment advisory firm. Through this kind of firm, I could manage my clients' money on the principles of long-term investing with no conflict of interest.

God gave me the assurance and peace that my move would be successful, but He did not promise me it would be easy. When I left the brokerage firm, I sent a letter to all my clients, hoping to transfer to my new firm about one-half of the $22 million I was managing for the brokerage firm. To my surprise, the brokerage firm threatened to take me to court, claiming that because I had originally signed a noncompete agreement with them, I could not serve any clients in my new firm that I had served in the brokerage firm.

The brokerage firm did not have a solid case against me—first because I had not signed a noncompete agreement at the time I was hired. Also, I had not had the advantage of legal representation when I signed the contract, and finally because the state of Georgia had ruled noncompete contracts unconstitutional. The brokerage firm knew this, but they wanted desperately to make an example of me so that no one else would leave the firm. They told my attorney they would move the case into federal court and have the judge issue a cease and desist order to shut down my business and source of income.

My attorney told me the firm knew they could not win in court, but they intended to tie me up in court for so long that they would ruin my new business. They had deep pockets, and my pockets, at the time, were very shallow. My attorney and I decided the best plan was for me to compromise with the firm. So, instead of starting a new business with $10 to $15 million in client accounts, I started with only a few hundred thousand dollars' worth of accounts. In other words, I was pretty much starting from scratch.

The first year was difficult for Angela and me. Our total combined gross income for 1994 was a mere $6,000. Angela was a full-time student in nursing, so she was not able to put much money into our pockets, and my new start-up business was suffering. Out of the $6,000 gross income in 1994, we gave God $3,000 and lived off the rest. So, our net income for 1994 after tithes, offerings and taxes was less than $3,000. But God made a way when there seemed to be no way. We were never late on any of our car payments, house payments or any other payments. We should have been devastated, but God met all our needs because we had been faithful in giving to Him. What God did for us, He will do for you.

Keep All God's Commandments

In my walk with the Lord, I have noticed that many Christians pluck scriptures out of the Bible to fit their immediate wants or needs, but they will not follow all of God's Word. The Bible uses the word *all* on many occasions when it tells us what we must do to be blessed of God. We read in Deuteronomy 28:1, "And it shall come to pass, if thou shalt hearken diligently unto the voice of the Lord thy God, to observe and to do *all* his commandments which I command thee this day, that the Lord thy God will set thee on high above all nations of the earth."

What Christians must realize is that all God's promises are conditional. If we do all He tells us, we will be blessed; however, if we do not do *all* God commands, if we follow His Word partially, God will not bless us.

- If Joshua had walked around the wall of Jericho six times instead of seven, then the walls would not have fallen.

- If Naaman had dipped six times in the Jordan River instead of seven times, he would not have been healed of leprosy.

- If David had charged the Philistine army instead of waiting for the shaking in the mulberry bush, he would have lost the battle.

- If Moses had not held his arms up in the battle in the wilderness, Israel would have lost the battle.

- If Jehoshaphat had not dug a ditch in the wilderness of Edom, the entire army of Judah and Israel would have been destroyed by the hand of the Moabites.

If God tells us to jump up and down for 15 minutes to get blessed, then we must jump 15 minutes, not 14 minutes, not an hour, but 15 minutes. We are to follow all God's Word completely.

Many Christians pay tithes and offerings, and yet they never seem to be blessed. Even though they have been faithful to pay their tithes, many are not blessed because they have failed to do other things God has commanded His children to do. For instance, God has called all Christians to be good stewards of what He has given them, and too many Christians are not very good stewards.

Be Good Stewards

We all are stewards of God's possessions, and God owns all things. A steward is not the owner; rather, he manages another's resources. Everything we own belongs to God, and we are to manage wisely what God has given us.

I fully understand this definition of stewardship. As a fee-only investment adviser, I am a steward of my clients' assets. If I do a good job, they will reward me by giving me more assets to manage. If I do poorly, then they will eventually remove their assets and entrust them to someone else. As Christians and believers in God's Word, we are supposed to be just, good and wise stewards of all God's possessions. Being a good steward is one of the requirements for opening the avenues of blessings; however, too many Christians ignore stewardship, or are simply ignorant of how to be a good steward.

I have heard Christians pray, "God, give me a new car." However, when I look at the car they have, I notice that it is not maintained—the oil is not changed, the tires are not rotated, and the car is not kept clean. I can imagine God asking, "Why should I give you a new car when you do not take care of the one you currently own?"

This question applies quite well to the rest of our finances. Why should God bless a man or woman who cannot manage what they currently have? If you cannot manage the $10,000 you have now, how can you be trusted to manage $1,000,000? We are called to be good stewards with all God has given us. If God finds us faithful in the small things, then He will bless us by giving us larger things to manage (Matthew 25:21). If God's Word gives us a commandment, we are to obey and not ask questions. As the Bible promises, if the believer will hearken and do ALL the Lord has commanded, then he and his house will be blessed. Amen.

Proclaim God's Promises

To be blessed of God, Christian believers must proclaim what they believe God is going to do for them. Usually we proclaim God's promises for the sake of others, as a form of witnessing. But this is not always the case. We also proclaim God's promises to write them in our own hearts. This principle is now widely recognized by psychologists and motivational thinkers.

Many years ago Napoleon Hill wrote a book called *Think and Grow Rich*, which the public thought to be a breakthrough on what to do to become rich, spiritually and materially. After I read the book, I discovered that many of the principles used in the book are based on the Bible. Hill is clearly in line with the Bible when he suggests that people daily repeat their goals and their strategies for obtaining these goals until the goals are embedded in their subconscious. He notes that for most people, the greatest barriers to success and personal fulfillment are self-created. In other words, something in their own mind and heart is stopping them from having the life they dream about. Repeating their goals daily, or proclaiming God's promises daily, can help them overcome the internal barriers to success.

Mission Possible

In the summer of 1994, during the time of extreme hardship for Angie and me, I had a vision while I was in a prayer meeting one Wednesday night. I know this vision was from God. I was fully awake, sitting in the pew three seats from the front of the sanctuary, when God stood me before a great wall, similar to the Great Wall of China. I looked left and right, but I could not see the beginning or the ending of this very thick wall. With a bat in my hand, I beat against the wall, but to no avail. It was as if the bat was made of plastic. When I could not move the great wall, a great hand from heaven came out of a cloud and gave me another bat. Taking the bat from the hand, I hit the wall one time and it opened. When I came out of the vision, I told no one of the experience. After the prayer meeting, I went home and got into my prayer closet to pray for God to give me the bat that blew the large hole in the wall. While I was praying, in the Spirit or in the flesh (I do not know), the word of the Lord came to me and said, "How about Jeremiah 23?" I kept praying, but the voice persisted: "How about Jeremiah 23?" When I could stand it no longer, I opened my Bible to Jeremiah 23, where I found the following words: "Is not my word like as a fire? saith the Lord; and like a hammer that breaketh the rock in pieces" (v. 29)? God was telling me that the mountains of opposition before me were not moveable by me alone; however, if I proclaimed God's Word in my life and spoke to the mountains, then the mountains would be removed.

So, now I speak to the mountains of opposition in my life. When I'm in financial hardship, I proclaim that God will supply all my needs according to His riches in glory and that He wishes for me to be prosperous even as my soul prospers. This is something I did not get out of a book; rather, it was revealed to me through the Spirit of God. We are to speak God's blessing in our life. We are to publicly proclaim God's promises for us. We are to speak them as if they are already done in our lives. Jesus says to speak unto the mountain, "Remove hence to yonder place; and it shall remove; and nothing shall be impossible unto you" (Matthew 17:20). Christ is teaching us to speak of things not as we see them, but as we know He sees them.

People may accuse us of lying to ourselves, but we are not. If we speak in faith and know that "faith is the substance of things hoped for, the evidence of things not seen" (Hebrews 11:1), then we are speaking of things hoped for and believing the evidence will appear by the God who rewards those who diligently seek Him. God tells us in His Word that His promises are yes and amen (2 Corinthians 1:20). God wills that we be blessed. So, we should proclaim that promise in our lives until our faith makes it a reality.

"Name-It-and-Claim-It" Theology

I first heard about name-it-and-claim-it theology back in the mid-70s when someone told a story about a man who went into his local Cadillac dealership proclaiming that the dealership was to give him a new top-of-the-line Cadillac as a gift from God. I do not recall if the fellow got the car, but after many years of studying God's Word, I suspect he did not.

The man was asking amiss for God's blessings. Rather than ask God to move the dealership to sacrifice and give him a free car (a winning situation for the man only), the fellow should have asked the Lord to bless him so that he could purchase the car himself (a winning situation for all involved). God's blessings benefit everyone. If the man had bought his own car, then both he and the car dealer would have been blessed of God. Rather, the man in this name-it-and-claim-it story is asking merely to satisfy his own desires for a new, expensive automobile. The Bible tells us in James 4:3, "Ye ask, and receive not, because ye ask amiss, that ye may consume it upon your lusts." God does not honor this kind of prayer.

Many of the pastors preaching name-it-and-claim-it theology promise that if we pay our tithes and offerings unto the Lord, He will shower us with financial blessings. They suggest that we do not have to work hard to be financially blessed, because God's will is not for us to work ourselves to death to obtain wealth.

While the promise sounds wonderful, all this doctrine actually delivers is laziness, which is totally contrary to God's Word. We are instructed to mark those who cause divisions and offenses contrary to the doctrine that we have learned, and to avoid those people (see Romans 16:17). After hearing many of these pastors preach, I get the impression that their definition of working yourself to death would be to work one hour over 40 hours per week. This type of theology would have been publicly derided and ridiculed 75 years ago, but as our country falls deeper into sin and gets softer, more of us seem to want something for nothing.

Unfortunately, too many of our pastors have embraced this new name-it-and-claim-it theology of accumulating wealth without working hard, and their teaching is ensnaring too many lazy Christians. Lazy Christians pay their tithes and offerings, but they do not work hard and smart for God. If they would work hard and smart, then God would have an open avenue through which to pour out His blessings on them. The false doctrine leads lazy Christians to believe that God will rain money, like manna, out of heaven; that they will mysteriously find checks in their mailbox; or that they will win the lottery. God does not work this way.

These Christians forget that they must do what the entire Bible teaches and not just what they select to read in a few scriptures. The name-it-and-claim-it preachers are correct about God's desire to bless us, but they are totally wrong when they suggest that we do not have to work hard to prepare ourselves for those blessings, to open the avenues to those blessings. God told Adam that henceforth he would earn his way by the sweat of his brow (Genesis 3:19), and it is no different for us than it was for Adam.

If you want to be better than the average person, you must do more than the average person. If you want to be more spiritual, you must pray, read your Bible and fast more. If you want to make and accumulate more wealth than average, you must work more. The secret to success is simple: Trust in God, be a good steward of what God has given you, and work hard. All of God's Word works in tandem; you cannot pull out a verse of Scripture and expect God to bless you if you do not adhere to all of God's Word. We are to be good stewards of God's time; we must work hard and smart and show God that we are responsible.

The Bible tells us that poverty will come to the lazy man (Proverbs 24:30-34), so we might well ask the name-it-and-claim-it person how God can bless the lazy Christian who will not wisely shepherd that which God has provided him. The short answer is that God will not bless such a person, because God keeps His word. We must do ALL that the Bible tells us if we are to be blessed of the Lord. Hebrews 6:12 tells us that Christians are not to be slothful, but they are to be full of faith and patience. These hardworking Christians, these faithful stewards, will inherit the promises of God.

Budgeting and Savings

As stated in the last chapter, the first step in being a good steward is to support God's church through the giving of our tithes and our time. The second step is to manage the money that God has provided for us. As the parable of the faithful servant showed us, if we cannot manage what God provides at first, then we cannot expect God to give us more.

Many Christians will pay tithes and give offerings to their church, but they will not budget and save money. I have Christian friends who eat out for lunch and dinner almost every day, but they never have any money in savings or in investments. These Christians are not being good stewards of what God has given them. They do not realize that if they cut back on the money they spend eating out one or two nights a week, they could save enough money to start on the road that leads to success.

Christians make up the body of Christ, but they have different tastes and preferences that affect their willingness to save and budget. Like most people, Christians enjoy excessive spending, and they justify their spending by saying, "Unlike most of the world, I don't drink alcohol, smoke tobacco or run around on my spouse, so

I should enjoy life. I deserve it." They spend their money on expensive meals, unnecessary clothing or new cars and feel comfortable because they are wasting their money on things that in themselves are not sinful. They don't see that they are not being good stewards of the riches God has provided and that they are closing off the avenues for further blessings.

They are not unlike the Prodigal Son in Luke 15:11-32, who wasted his money on riotous living and an excessive lifestyle. Popular thought says that the Prodigal Son wasted his wealth on a sinful life, but the Bible story does not say that. The Bible says the younger son turned the whole of his share into cash and left home for a distant country, where he squandered it in reckless living (see v. 13). Like the Prodigal Son, too many Christians are squandering their wealth in reckless living, not sinning, but squandering their wealth nonetheless.

What is so unfortunate is that most Christians do not realize they are living recklessly. They do not realize that the money they spend on eating out, buying new clothes and cars is excess money that they could be turning into God's blessings. They convince themselves that they are purchasing necessities. However, if they learned to budget their finances, these Christians would soon find out that they have excess money that could be saved and invested, turned into a blessing from God.

Planning for Wealth

Planning is the first step in the budgeting and saving process. You do not have a plan until you write down your short and long-term goals, defining your objectives and the parameters necessary to meet those objectives. Writing down your goals makes them more obtainable. It also solidifies the commitment you have made to yourself, your family and God. When written down, your goals are no longer just dreams. Studies show that you are four times as likely to achieve a goal if you write it down. Institutions around the country use an Investment Policy Statement (IPS) that clearly

Budgeting and Savings

defines the investment goals of the institution and the resources the institution will invest to meet those goals. The value of written goals are so recognized that pension fiduciaries are required by law to maintain a goal statement at all times.

The first step in this planning process is to set long-term goals, because setting long-term goals first makes it easier to set intermediate goals later. Your long-term goals must be specific, measurable and finite, and they must be grounded in your love for Jesus Christ. For instance, you might write a goal such as, "Within five years, I will be tithing $15,000 a year to my local church." Note that this goal is specific and measurable and has a deadline, yet it is also founded on your love for Jesus Christ, for you are to love Him with all your heart, all your soul and all your might.

The second step in this planning process is to write down intermediate goals, which are the basic steps that lead to accomplishing long-term goals.

Then you break long-term goals into smaller tasks. How do you start tithing $15,000 a year? You don't. You start by tithing $2,000 or $4,000 or $8,000 a year, with plans to increase each year until you can achieve $15,000 a year. For example, you might plan to work 10 hours overtime each week until you build your business to $1,000,000 a year of gross sales. You are to work toward your goals each day and evaluate your progress periodically. Proverbs 29:18 says, "Where there is no vision, the people perish." You must set goals and have a vision of where you are going. Below is an example of a set of goals a small-business owner may strive to achieve.

- *Long-term goal*: To create a successful sales practice five years from today with revenues of $500,000 or more.

- *Intermediate goal*: For each year for the next five years, I will increase my revenues by $100,000.

- *Weekly goal*: Sale $1,925 of products weekly.

- *Daily goal*: Sale $385 of products daily.

Mission Possible

- *Daily and weekly tasks to meet my intermediate goals*:

  1. Meet five new people each week and tell them about the services of my company.

  2. Join new organizations and social clubs to meet new prospects to introduce to my service.

  3. Ask my existing clients for referrals on a quarterly basis.

  4. Conduct monthly seminars explaining my products and services.

  5. Ask my existing clients for new business.

  6. Advertise my products and services in the local paper weekly.

  7. Advertise my products in the yellow pages.

Creating a Budget

An effective written plan must be based on reality. The reality of your financial situation at any given time can be summarized in a document called a budget. A written budget tells you where you are financially, how much you are spending, and how much you should be spending based on your income. For many people the word *budget* means scrimping on their finances. It sounds cheap; however, the results of living on a budget are anything but cheap. You know where your money is going, and your budget builds financial success that leads to accumulated wealth.

Keep in mind that a budget is a 12-month, 365-days-a-year effort. Anything less, and the budget will not work. Excuses such as "It's Christmas" or "It's my birthday" do not give you permission to abandon your budget. Because a budget is so demanding, it is the part of accumulating wealth that people dislike the most.

My wife, Angela, hates budgeting. When we started a budget, Angela was not sold on the idea. She thought it would be too much

Budgeting and Savings

trouble, so I told her I would handle it. "Just be sure to keep all your receipts when you make your purchases," I told her.

I started our budget by recording in my computer everything we were spending. I decided I would enter data for the previous 12 months, so I could see where our money went over the past year and form some idea about how to trim our expenses for the coming year. This revealed that my wife and I were removing too much cash from our checking account and not accounting for where or how we spent it. It also revealed that we were spending entirely too much money for nonessential items such as knick-knacks and whatnots. I quickly formulated a plan for tracking our spending habits and cutting out the knick-knacks. We were soon able to start saving money to build wealth.

Many financial planners have a model budget that suggests you spend a certain percentage of your income for housing, transportation, food, and so forth. These percentages are just guidelines and will vary from house to house, but they do give you a place to start. An inexpensive computer program such as Microsoft *Money* or *Quicken* will help you track every financial transaction from credit cards, debit cards, checking, savings and investments. They will also generate budgets that show your cash flow, spending habits, taxes and investment statements. But you don't have to have a computer to create and keep a budget. You can do it the old-fashioned way with pen and paper. The important thing is to begin, and you begin by determining your available income.

1. *Determine your net income.* The first thing you need to do is determine how much money you have to budget, or your net income. Net income is figured by taking your total gross income minus taxes and pretax retirement plan contributions if you have a retirement plan.

Consider the example of Joseph and Rachel. Joseph is a broker at a local commodities firm and Rachel is employed as a child care specialist. Neither Joseph nor Rachel has a company-sponsored

Mission Possible

retirement plan. Joseph's total gross income is $52,000 per year, and Rachel's total gross income is $32,000 per year. Their combined total gross income is $84,000 per year.

To figure their monthly net income, divide their total gross income by 12 (12 months in a year), or $84,000/12 = $7,000. In both Joseph's and Rachel's case, they have 28 percent of their gross income withheld in federal, state and Social Security taxes ($7,000 x .28 = $1,960), which leaves them with $5,040 after taxes ($7,000 - $1,960 = $5,040). This $5,040 is their net income for the month, and it is the starting point we will use to figure a budget for them. When you start a budget, you should figure your income in the same way.

2. *List your expenditures.* As should all Christians, Joseph and Rachel first figure God into their budget. For the purpose of this illustration, we will figure tithes on their net income. Thus, Joseph and Rachel will tithe $504 per month ($5,040 x .10 = $504). Joseph and Rachel will also give an average of $100 per month to missions and offerings. After tax and charitable donations, they have $4,436 ($5,040 - $504 - $100 = $4,436).

From this point, Joseph and Rachel need to deduct all the expenses associated with their automobiles. Joseph's Chevrolet is paid off; however, the Honda that Rachel is leasing costs $405 per month. The gas, insurance, taxes and maintenance for the two autos cost $275, for a total of $680 in transportation costs per month.

Another costly item for this couple is their home. Housing expenses include mortgage or rent, insurance, taxes, electricity, natural gas, water, sanitation, telephone and maintenance. The couple also have a home equity line on which they currently owe $16,400, and their monthly loan payment is $250. They spend a total of $1,260 per month on housing.

Food is another necessity. They are currently spending $400 per month on groceries. Because they both work, they don't always want to cook, so Joseph and Rachel eat out frequently, which costs them about $105 per month. Their total food cost is $505 per month.

Recurring bills such as electricity, natural gas, telephone, water,

Budgeting and Savings

sewage and sanitation cost $215 per month. Since Joseph and Rachel are still young (Joseph is 37 years old and Rachel is 32), each is purchasing a $250,000 face value 10-year level term life insurance. This insurance costs them a total of $30 per month. The family medical insurance costs $285 per month. Their total monthly cost for insurance is $315.

Joseph and Rachel have been pretty good about not spending too much on credit cards. They currently owe $3,500 on all their credit cards with a monthly payment of $125. The bank charges $10 per month service charge on their checking account, for a total monthly payment for all debts of $135.

This past year Joseph and Rachel took a few short vacations and spent an average of $100 per month on travel. Rachel joined the YMCA to get back in shape after their second child was born, and the monthly health club fee is $35. The couple visit their parents once a month, spending an average of $25 per trip. Their total entertainment and recreation expense is $160 per month.

Other expenses include $40 per month for cable TV and a subscription to *Better Homes and Gardens* that costs about $5 per month. Joseph loves to go online and get the latest sports scores on the Internet, which costs $20 per month. The money they spend on their children in games and sports is $25 per month.

Their total clothing cost is $300 per month, plus $300 per month for school/child care for their 4- and 5-year-old children.

Joseph and Rachel have started a savings and investment plan and they save and invest $500 per month.

Our couple believes in the divine healing of Jesus Christ, and their total medical expense is $60 per month. This includes medical and dental bills.

From time to time miscellaneous items, such as cosmetics, gifts, lunches and entertainment must be purchased. This category includes all the expenses that do not fit in one of the above categories and totals $185 per month. Even a quick look at the totals for Joseph and Rachel's budget reveal that they are in trouble.

EXAMPLE
Joseph & Rachel
Illustration 1

Budget Worksheet

Gross Income Per Month	**$7,000.00**
Minus Federal Tax	$1,050.00
Minus FICA	$405.00
Minus Medicare	$95.00
Minus State Tax	$410.00
Minus Local Tax	
Minus Retirement Plan Contributions (401K, 403-B, etc.)	
Minus Health Insurance	
Minus Life Insurance	
Minus Flexible Spending Account (Medical)	
Minus Flexible Spending Account (Dependent Care)	
Minus Garnishments	
Total Net Income	$5,040.00

Expenses

Charitable Donations

Tithes	$504.00
Offerings	$60.00
Missions	$40.00
Other	
Total Charitable Donations	$604.00
Budget Guide	12%
Difference	**0.00**

Budgeting and Savings

Automobile
Car Payment/Lease	405.00
Gasoline and Oil	75.00
Maintenance	15.00
Parts	10.00
Insurance	135.00
Taxes	40.00
Total Automobile Expense	680.00
Budget Guide	13%
Difference	**-24.00**

Housing
Mortgage/Rent	715.00
Second Mortgage	250.00
Insurance	65.00
Taxes	130.00
Maintenance	35.00
Furnishing	25.00
Yard Service	40.00
Other	
Total Housing Expense	1,260.00
Budget Guide	25%
Difference	**0.00**

Food
Groceries	400.00
Dining Out	105.00
Total Food Expense	505.00
Budget Guide	9%
Difference	**-51.00**

Recurring Bills
Electricity	85.00
Natural Gas	40.00

Mission Possible

Telephone	45.00
Water and Sewage	30.00
Sanitation	15.00
Other	
Total Recurring Bills	215.00
Budget Guide	4%
Difference	**-13.00**

Insurance (omit if paid pretax through company)

Life	30.00
Medical	285.00
Disability	
Long-term Care	
Other	
Total Insurance Expense	315.00
Budget Guide	7%
Difference	**+38.00**

Debts

Credit Cards	125.00
Loans and Notes	
Bank Charges	10.00
Other	
Total Debts Expense	135.00
Budget Guide	3%
Difference	**+16.00**

Recreation and Entertainment

Activities and Trips	25.00
Vacation	100.00
Health Club	35.00
Social Club	
Other	
Total Recreation and Entertainment Expense	160.00

Budgeting and Savings

Budget Guide	2%
Difference	**-59.00**

Leisure

Books and Magazines	5.00
Cable	40.00
Sporting Goods	15.00
Toys and Games	10.00
Internet Expense	20.00
Total Leisure Expense	90.00
Budget Guide	2%
Difference	**+11.00**

Clothing

Total Clothing Expense	300.00
Budget Guide	2%
Difference	**-200.00**

Child Care

Day Care	
Baby-Sitter	50.00
School Tuition	240.00
Materials	10.00
School Transportation	
Children's Club	
Total Child Care Expense	300.00
Budget Guide	6%
Difference	**+2.00**

Savings and Investments

Total Savings and Investments	500.00
Budget Guide	10%
Difference	**+4.00**

Health Care
Dental	25.00
Hospital	
Physician	25.00
Drugs	10.00
Other	
Total Health Care Expense	60.00
Budget Guide	2%
Difference	**+39.00**

Miscellaneous
Photos	
Pet Care	
Advertising	
Beauty Supplies	25.00
Haircuts	25.00
Personal Care	5.00
Gifts	100.00
Laundry	
Cash	30.00
All Other Expenses Not Mentioned	
Total Miscellaneous Expense	185.00
Budget Guide	3%
Difference	**-34.00**

TOTAL OF ALL EXPENSES	**5,309.00**
Net Income	5,040.00
Less Expenses	5,309.00
Balance	-269.00
Difference	**-269.00**

Budgeting and Savings

As you can see by this example, Joseph and Rachel need to start living within their budget. They are spending $269 more a month than they are earning. Instead of spending $505 for food, which consists of $105 for dining out, they need to eat more at home and to cut their food expenses $51 a month. They need to dramatically trim their clothing budget and slightly trim their entertainment and recreation spending. This couple's budget and budget guide are laid out on Worksheet 3.

3. *Live within your budget.* All Christians need to learn to live within their budget. It is mandatory that Christians pay their taxes and tithes, save and invest at least 10 percent of what they make, and live on the rest. If you cannot live on the rest, you are living higher than your means. Jesus tells us of the parable of the tower in Luke 14:28-30, "For which of you, intending to build a tower, sitteth not down first, and counteth the cost, whether he have sufficient to finish it? Lest haply, after he hath laid the foundation, and is not able to finish it, all that behold it begin to mock him, saying, this man began to build, and was not able to finish."

Many Christians begin to live and spend without counting the cost. Many fall into financial hardship because they did not budget their spending, and then are dismayed when the world mocks them for not counting the cost. The Bible tells us that the man who thinks and plans will increase in abundance. Proverbs 21:5 says, "The thoughts of the diligent tend only to plenteousness; but of every one that is hasty only want." The man who does not plan and count the cost will not succeed. *Worksheet 4* (appendix, p. 148) has the basic guidelines for doing a budget.

Seeds of Financial Security

To have money for investments so that you can accumulate wealth, you must first be able to save money. The only reason this chapter on budgeting and saving is in this book is to warn you that if you are not able to budget and save, you are closing the avenues

Mission Possible

through which God can bless you financially. If you cannot save money, then stop reading now. This book will be nothing but a prediction of continued financial bondage.

Your savings are the seeds of your financial independence. The Bible often talks about the seed as the potential of what will be. Galatians 6:7 says, "Be not deceived; God is not mocked: for whatsoever a man soweth, that shall he also reap." If you sow apple seeds, you will not reap oranges. If you sow love, you will reap love. Likewise, if you sow money, you will reap money. Simply put, money makes money, and if you have no seed to sow because you wasted it on wasteful living, you will reap nothing.

And you should not expect to reap anything. I often hear Christians pray, "Lord, give me more money so that I can have this or that new gadget." Unfortunately, most Christians do not understand that the key to wealth is not how much money they make, but how much money they save. Too many Christians simply increase their lifestyle when they receive a raise in pay; thus, in a short time, their lifestyle spending has increased, but they are still in financial bondage.

People tend to live up to their means. I know of a Christian fellow who was making $9 per hour, when he prayed that the Lord would give him a better job so that he could get out of financial bondage. The Lord opened the door, and the guy now has a job that is paying him $18 per hour. The sad thing is this Christian's spending has increased, and he still is in financial bondage. He has not learned that the key to wealth is not how much you make but how much you save.

I once read a story of a woman who was employed by the Internal Revenue Service as an auditor. This woman died in the mid-1990s at age 103. At age 50, she had started investing in quality stocks, saying that she had noticed that the wealthy individuals and families she audited all owned stocks. This woman never made more than $3,500 a year her entire working life. Her family never left her an inheritance. She never married a rich man. She never won the lottery. However, she did live well within her means, she did put aside a bit

Budgeting and Savings

of money each month, and she did purchase quality stocks for 50 years. At her death, her stock portfolio was worth more than $100 million. Her philosophy was to buy and hold high-quality stocks, a well-known investment strategy, but what made it possible was her recognition that the key to wealth is not what she made, but what she saved and invested.

All Christians should save money on a regular basis. Those who are below the level of poverty should pray that they will obtain a better job so that they can start saving on a regular basis. It is not God's will for a Christian to live in poverty. We know this from God's Word, which tells us in 3 John 2, "Beloved, I wish above all things that thou mayest prosper and be in health, even as thy soul prospereth." Many other scriptures tell us that it is not God's will for us to be in poverty, but it is His will that we live within our means. If we do so, we will have extra money to invest.

Christians should strive to invest at least 10 percent of their gross income. However, consider the example of the wisest man who ever lived, Solomon, who was chosen by God to build the Temple of the Lord in Jerusalem. First Kings 6:38 says that it took the builders seven years to build the Temple. And when it was completed, Solomon invested almost twice as much time and money into his own house as he had invested in the house of the Lord. The same builders who had built the Temple took almost 13 years to build the house of King Solomon (see 1 Kings 7:1). The important thing to notice is that God never rebuked King Solomon for this extravagance. God commands us to give Him 10 percent, but why should we not be wise and follow King Solomon's footsteps and invest and save 20 percent of what we earn? This should be the savings goal for all Christians.

4

Investing and Accumulating Wealth

Now is the right time to begin accumulating wealth. Be a good steward of God's time. The earlier a Christian starts the investment process, the easier it is to accumulate wealth. For instance, a 20-year-old Christian who invests $167 per month, or $2,000 per year, into a good quality no-load mutual fund that yields a 10 percent annualized rate of return will have invested a total of $90,000 at age 65. Ten percent per year is about what the Standard & Poors 500 returned over the past 100 years. So, 10 percent is a realistic return. The investment would have grown to a staggering $1.4 million, before taxes.

This simple illustration does not take into consideration that as the investor ages and becomes more established, he should be able to invest more money. If the same Christian decides to wait until he reaches age 40 to start investing, the same $167 per month will grow only to $196,000. So, the amount of time invested is crucial to success. Time is on your side; but start the investing process as soon as possible.

The wise Christian investor (CI)[1] will take advantage of this. Do not get discouraged if you're getting close to retirement but have not

---
[1] Hereafter, CI will refer to Christian investor.

started investing and accumulating wealth. The mission is still possible. It will just take a little more effort. Warren Buffett said, "To invest successfully over a lifetime does not require a stratospheric IQ, unusual business insights or inside information. What's needed is sound intellectual framework for making decisions and the ability to keep emotions from corroding that framework."

Getting Started

The first thing the CI must do is open a brokerage account. The process is very simple, much like opening a bank account. Fill out a few forms and decide on the type of brokerage firm—a full-service brokerage firm or a discount brokerage. After you have read this book and followed its guidelines, you should be able to bypass the full-service broker stage and go directly with a discount broker.

Forget the lowest commission firms and find a firm that will give you good service and quality executions of trades. My investment advisory firm currently uses Charles Schwab as our custodian (discount broker). Fidelity, Jack White and TD Waterhouse are also well-established discount brokerage firms. Many of these established firms will allow you to trade via Internet for even lower commission rates. If you decide to go the Internet route, be very careful. Double-check when you type in the security symbols and quantities. Some investors will think they purchased Microsoft (symbol "MSFT") when they accidentally bought Microstrategy (symbol "MSTR"). I know of other investors who intended to purchase 100 shares of a company, but inadvertently hit an extra zero and purchased 1,000 shares of the company. I would suggest that you start by opening a cash account at the discount brokerage firm of your choice. You must spend at least several hours each week keeping track of your investments and the general stock market. The learning curve can be fast if you spend time studying the market.

In the past, major brokerage firms would employ a person and have the person study three months in order to pass the series seven General Securities exam. After the person passed the exam, the firm would train him/her for about six weeks. When the six-week time period was over, he/she was a full-blown stockbroker, account executive and financial consultant. So, in four and one-half months the firm would have a new employee managing the money of wealthy individuals. For smaller regional brokerage firms, the time period was even less. For a Christian willing to work and study the stock market, the learning curve can be extremely fast.

Mutual Funds and Common Stocks

A new CI does not need a lot of money to start. A minimum of $500 will get you started in a good quality mutual fund. It's hard to beat individual stocks and growth funds for long-term growth of capital. Historically, common stocks have consistently outperformed all other investments. This includes real estate, art, coins, corporate and government bonds, CDs, and money markets. Also, common stocks have kept investors well ahead of inflation, making them a good hedge against inflation.

As a long-term Christian investor, inflation is one of your greatest enemies. Rising prices of goods and services can destroy your future financial security by eroding your future purchasing power. Even a relatively modest rate of inflation can seriously diminish purchasing power. For example, if inflation is running at 4 percent a year, $1,000 will be worth only $665 in 10 years. Similarly, if the return on your investments barely beat inflation, you will just scantily keep up with rising prices. To come out ahead in the long run, your investments must significantly outpace inflation. Mutual funds can be a smart way to harness the long-term growth potential of stocks. Many good quality no-load mutual funds have a minimum of $1,000. And some of these funds will lower the minimum if the client guarantees to start a dollar cost averaging plan with the fund. This plan is when the client decides to make direct electronic deposits from his/her checking or savings account into a mutual fund. Some Christians may even opt for mailing a check rather than having their funds electronically transferred.

Mission Possible

Dollar cost averaging is a wonderful way for the inexperienced Christian to start investing. Simply put, a mutual fund is a pool of investors' dollars. The money is used to purchase a diversified portfolio of stocks, bonds or money market instruments under the continuous supervision of professional managers. Mutual funds seek to do for investors what they might do for themselves if they had the time, inclination, background, experience and resources to spread investments among many securities. Each investor shares in the fund's income, expenses, profits and losses in proportion to the number of shares owned.

Think of a mutual fund kind of like a pie. Many ingredients go into the pie: sugar, flour, milk, shortening, flavoring. A mutual fund is very similar: shares of Coke, Motorola, Wal-Mart and Treasury bonds are examples of the ingredients that make the mutual fund. When you purchase a mutual fund, you are buying a slice of the pie. If the money manager has the right ingredients, the fund will increase; however, if the money manager has bad ingredients, the fund will perform poorly. The taste of the pie depends on the ingredients the cook puts in it. The performance of the fund will be determined by the investments placed in the fund.

Now, back to dollar cost averaging. What is so great about this type of investing is that market conditions work for you, not against you. Regular, periodic purchases, of the same dollar amount each week, month or quarter, will render more shares of a fund when its price is low and fewer shares when its price is high. Thus, the average share price will be averaged down, reducing the risk of putting money into stocks at the top of the market. No-load funds are the ideal vehicle for employing the dollar cost averaging strategy because there is no sales charge on purchases, thus *all* the money goes to work for you.

I started a dollar cost averaging plan as soon as I graduated college. I was looking to invest small amounts of money into an aggressive mutual fund; the Twentieth Century Ultra Fund fit my risk tolerance. Starting with $500, I invested $50 a month into the

Investing and Accumulating Wealth

fund. In addition to the $50 per month, each time the market would make a pull back of about 10 percent, I would scrape up some extra money to add to the fund. In a short period of time, my dollar cost averaging portfolio had grown to $6,000. I later used this money to buy an engagement ring for my wife.

In building the framework, a CI must calculate his or her risk tolerances and investment objectives. In this book, the term *risk* is used in a broad sense to refer to deviations from expectations. Christian investors need to be aware of the amount of risk they are willing to take with their money, and then they need to find investments that are consistent with that risk tolerance. In building this foundation and framework, our risk tolerances and investment objectives will be our cornerstone—just like Jesus Christ is our chief cornerstone (see Ephesians 2:20).

After reading this book, the CI should be able to discover with certainty the measure of each fund's risk and to identify the investments that have historically been best at providing investors with returns commensurate with the risk taken. The risk of an investment portfolio can be calculated just like the return on a portfolio can be calculated. The risk of an investment is based on its volatility. The more variable the investment (up and down), the wider the swings in price, the riskier the investment. Generally speaking, stocks are riskier than fixed-income investments and, for that reason, provide greater rewards. Research by Ibbotson Associates indicates that over the long-term (75 years), an 11.0 percent total return on stocks can be expected. After inflation, the real return on stocks is a hair above 7 percent annually. Fixed-income investments averaged just 5.7 percent annually, only a hair above 2.5 percent over inflation.

In mutual funds, stocks and investment portfolios, *beta* is a measure of the variability of a single security or portfolio of assets relative to some market measure, such as the Standard & Poors 500 stock index. In other words, the *beta* of a security will measure the sensitivity to market movements of a single investment or a portfolio of investments. By definition, the beta of the benchmark index is 1.00.

So, if a mutual fund has a beta of 1.2, the mutual fund would be 20 percent riskier than the stock market, and thus would be expected to perform 20 percent better than the index in a good market and 20 percent worse in down markets. If the beta of a mutual fund were .50, the investment would have half the risk of the stock market and would be expected to perform 50 percent less than the index in up markets and 50 percent better in down markets.

Illustration 2

[Chart showing investment A and investment B performance from 1yr to 5yr, ranging from -5% to 12%]

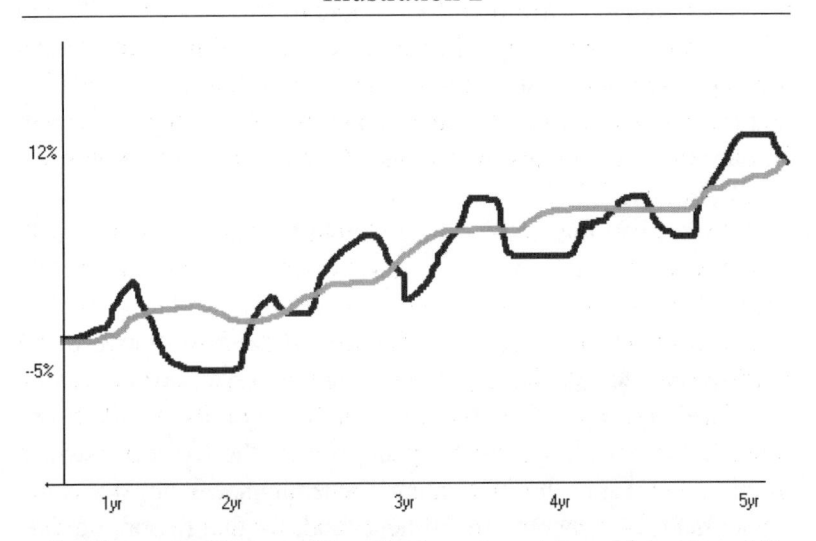

In *Illustration 2* you will notice investment A and investment B. Both of these investments have had the same return over a five-year period; both have averaged 12 percent. However, the wise CI would have chosen investment A over investment B. The volatility of investment B is greater than that of investment A, yet the investments have the same annual return. When evaluating two mutually exclusive investments having approximately equal net present values, the investor should choose the less risky investment. Thus, the risk / reward ratio is greater with investment A. The investor would have taken less risk with investment A; however, his return would have been equal to investment B.

Investing and Accumulating Wealth

A wise CI will look for investments that generate superior returns with less risk. Notice how in year two, in *Illustration 2*, if the investor would have been forced out of this investment due to some unexpected circumstances, he would have suffered a loss if he had invested in investment B. Investment A, on the other hand, has had very small fluctuations over the same five-year time period; and if the investor would have been forced out in year two, he still would have had a good return on his investment. These fluctuations can be mathematically computed to give us an idea of the risk of an investment.

Taking Risks

Over the past 15 years, many potential investors have come into my office desiring a stock or mutual fund that will fly to the moon and have absolutely zero risk. I hate to break the news to these naive investors, but no such investment exists. I feel compelled to remind them that God's Word never mentions taking too much risk as being sinful. On the contrary, He states *not* taking risk is a sin.

Consider Matthew 25:14-30. The lord of the three servants gave talents (money) to each servant according to his ability. Two of the servants took on some risk and doubled their master's money; however, the third servant who was not willing to risk his lord's money buried his money in the ground. The two who were willing to risk loss for potential gain doubled the lord's money and were rewarded for their good deeds. The wicked and slothful servant, who was not willing to risk his lord's money, had the money taken away and given to the one with the greatest ability. The lord of the house rebuked the man for not taking any risk and told him he could have at least taken his money to the banker and earned interest on it.

This parable of the talents is a prime example of instructing Christians to invest their money for profits. Many Christians say, "I'm not going to gamble my money. I'm putting my little bit of money into a Certificate of Deposit at the local bank where it is not at risk." Well, shortsightedness of this nature is sad, unless these folks always want to have just a little money. Like the wicked and slothful servant, they wonder why God does not open the windows of heaven so they will not have room enough to receive. The answer is simple: They are not being a good steward of God's money. To be blessed of God, we have to obey all His commandments. So, taking on some calculated risk is a necessity if we are going to be blessed of God.

Christians often ask me, "Is investing in stocks and mutual funds the same as gambling?" The answer is no! Here's why. Gambling is taking an extraordinary amount of risk for an above-average gain. *Merriam-Webster's Collegiate Dictionary,* Tenth Edition, defines *gambling* as follows: "to bet on an uncertain outcome; to take a chance." A gambler may risk $1 hoping to win $500. Everything we do in a sense involves risk with some possible reward for the risk taken. For example, there is risk associated with driving an automobile to the grocery store. Statistics tell us that the majority of traffic fatalities happen within a couple blocks of home. The risk of driving a couple blocks to the grocery store is the possibility of a traffic fatality. The reward is dinner on the table. Gambling is inherent in the human psyche. However, the Bible never teaches us that we should never take a risk. God's Word does teach us not to desire quick riches (Proverbs 28:20) and to abstain from all appearance of evil (1 Thessalonians 5:22). If God's Word were to teach against taking huge amounts of risk, where would God draw the line and tell us that any amount of risk above this line is sin? God in His infinite wisdom gives us the ability to calculate risks with good judgment, so we can make the right investment choices.

Investing Objectives

Investing, by definition, is the purchase of an asset expected—not assured—to provide a return in the future. Investing is taking a calculated risk for an expected gain. The great investor Warren Buffett said, "Risk comes from not knowing what you are doing." After reading this book, the CI will know what to do.

Investing and Accumulating Wealth

Look now at *Worksheet 1* (appendix, p. 141) and fill out and grade the questionnaire to determine how much calculated risk you should be willing to take on your investment portfolio. After grading the questionnaire, determine if you should be investing in a conservative, moderate or aggressive portfolio. A conservative mutual fund will have a beta of .70 or less. A moderate risk portfolio will have a beta of .71 to 1.10. Anything with a beta greater than 1.10 is considered an aggressive portfolio.

What a CI must know is that an aggressive mutual fund in a conservative or moderate portfolio is satisfactory, as long as the total sum of the portfolio's beta does not create another risk category. In other words, any category of mutual fund in your portfolio will work as long as the beta of the entire portfolio remains in the predetermined risk category range. For example, after filling out the questionnaire, you scored in the conservative risk category and now have a total of $25,000 to invest. So your investment portfolio should have a beta of .70 or less. This simply means that your portfolio will be a minimum of 30 percent less volatile than the stock market.

A conservative portfolio may look like this:

Percentage Distribution	Fund	Beta
15 percent	Artisan Mid Cap fund	1.13
25 percent	Scudder Greater Europe	.60
30 percent	Schwab 1000	1.01
30 percent	Cohen & Steers Realty	.25

As you have probably noticed, this portfolio has two funds of moderate or aggressive risk growth mutual funds; however the beta for the entire portfolio is only .75. This portfolio will be 30 percent less risky than the stock market, a conservative portfolio. Hardly a gamble. Morningstar, the mutual fund rating service, offers yet another unique way of measuring risk. Unlike beta, which takes into account up and downside risk, Morningstar assigns its risk percentile

Mission Possible

ranking called *stars*, which evaluates the fund's downside risk only. Funds are compared to other funds in their class. Morningstar believes that most investors' greatest fear is losing money. *Downside risk* is defined as underperforming the three-month Treasury bill return. So, Morningstar's star ratings focus only on downside risk. This star rating is expressed on a scale of 1 to 5 stars. This risk-adjusted rating has one star as being the worst and five stars as being the best. Morningstar's risk-adjusted star rating should be used as an initial screen and not a conclusion.

Many investors do not consider a mutual fund's Sharpe ratio when purchasing a mutual fund. Nobel Laureate William Sharpe developed this ratio, and it can be an excellent way to quantify a fund's risk-adjusted performance. This ratio will show the investor the relationship between excess return and risk. What the Christian investor must know about the Sharpe ratio is that the higher the ratio, the better the fund's historical risk-adjusted performance.

After determining risk tolerances and investment objects, the next step is to start selecting mutual funds for your portfolio. There are over 6,000 mutual funds with a wide range of objectives for investors to choose from. They vary enormously in performance, so picking the wrong fund can be costly. With Christians being called of God to be wise and not foolish, they must do their homework and choose the correct investments for their investment goals and risk tolerances. It requires time and know-how, but once you learn the fundamentals, your periodic review will take no longer than a couple hours per month.

For the CI to go through the selection process speedily, he or she first must be able to match funds to the appropriate investment objectives. At one end of the spectrum are funds committed to conservative investing. These funds are entrusted to conserve capital and produce income. At the other extreme are funds that invest speculatively for maximum capital gains. All other funds fall somewhere in the middle.

Investing and Accumulating Wealth

Illustration 3
Risk/Reward

Appropriate Fund:	Money Market	Fixed Income	Balanced	Income and Growth	Growth	Aggressive Growth

⟵—————————————————————————————⟶
Low risk					High risk

Investor's Objective:	Liquidity	Stable Yield	Income	Conservative Growth	Moderate Growth	Aggressive Growth

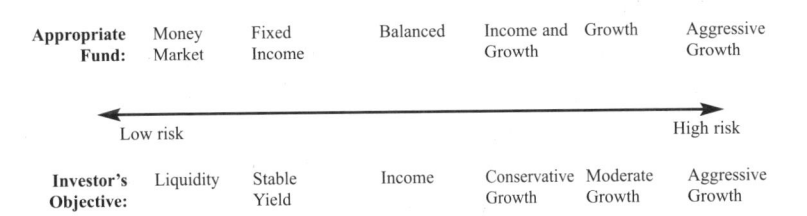

Illustration 3 graphically depicts the spectrum in a straight line. Conservative funds are on the far left and aggressive funds are on the far right. By knowing which type of fund lines up with your investment objectives, the CI can cut the time spent analyzing mutual funds. For example, if you fall into an aggressive risk-growth category, there is no reason to spend much time analyzing long-term bond funds.

There are five general classes of mutual funds. Money market funds are excluded, because they are more of a savings instrument. The list starts with the most speculative fund category and proceeds down the risk spectrum.

1. *Aggressive growth funds* are not for the fainthearted. These funds invest for the greatest possible gains. They are also known as small-company growth funds, maximum capital gains funds, micro-cap funds, emerging markets funds, capital appreciation funds and performance funds. The objective of an aggressive growth fund is to grow faster than all other funds by whatever means it takes to get there. Some characteristics of aggressive growth funds are as follows:

- They try to obtain maximum capital gains.

- To achieve these gains, they take on large amounts of risk.

- These funds are volatile, doing well in good markets, terrible in bad markets.

- They may occasionally use even more speculative ways of obtaining capital gains, such as buying on margin, short selling and options.

2. *Growth funds* are long-term growth funds intended to grow your money steady over longer periods of time. Growth funds on average do not employ the speculative ploys that aggressive growth funds use to obtain maximum capital gains. These funds are more likely to hold well-established companies, such as the companies that make up the Dow Jones 30 and the Standard & Poors 500. Some of these funds will seek well-known companies and some smaller, lesser-known companies. These funds are usually more consistent with their returns. They are volatile but much less volatile than aggressive growth funds.

3. *Growth and income funds* aim to give investors capital appreciation with some income. These funds usually hold stocks with higher yields than growth funds. Stocks that pay higher dividend yields are considered more conservative than lower dividend paying stocks. The old thought behind this is that established companies are willing to pay more of their earnings to shareholders, while start-up companies and companies trying to get established use their earnings to grow. Typically, a growth and income fund's primary objective is growth; income is their secondary objective.

4. *Balanced funds* are the most conservative funds that invest in stocks. They typically will have about half of their portfolio in income-producing stocks and the remainder in other income-producing investments.

5. *Bond funds* invest in a portfolio of interest bearing bonds. Unlike individual bonds that have a stated maturity, bond funds do not mature. When considering a bond fund, an investor should examine the average maturity dates of the bonds in the fund. The longer the maturity, the higher the risk. A bond duration is also a useful tool in evaluating a bond. *Duration* is the average number of years it takes to

Investing and Accumulating Wealth

receive the present value of all future payments. If considering two similar bond funds with similar maturities, choose the bond fund with the lowest duration. When considering a bond fund, do not look just at yield. Consider the total return of the bond fund. These are some of the major bond categories: corporate bond funds, GNMA funds, high-yield or junk bond funds, flexible bond funds, international bond funds, zero-coupon bond funds, government bond funds, and municipal bond or tax-free bond funds.

Summary
1. Determine your risk tolerances and investment objectives by filling out the questionnaire (appendix, p. 141).
2. Open up a brokerage account at a discount brokerage firm.
3. Familiarize yourself with the various types of mutual funds.

5

The Selection Process

Up to this point, the CI has determined the risk tolerances and investment objectives. He or she is familiar with the five categories of mutual funds and how they differ. So the next step is learning how to pick the best mutual funds in each category. By far the most important factor is past performance; we will also look at securities turnover, fund expenses, size, fund family and fund managers.

Past Performance

Mutual fund advertisements warn that past performance is not a guarantee of future results. This is true. However, past performance is used as a major predictor of future results. This is not a conflict in statements, because past performance has been the best-proven way of forecasting future results. It is not cut in stone, but it is superior to all other ways of forecasting future results. So, past performance will be the major criteria we will use in selecting our mutual funds. With that in mind, increase your chances of picking a winner by choosing the best past time periods to examine.

Mission Possible

CIs should look at one year, three-year and five-year time periods. Most mutual funds today are not 10 years old, so considering a 10-year track record is not practical. What time periods make the most sense greatly depends on how the investor forecasts the future. In the last stages of a bear market (a market that is gone down 30 percent from its high) where the future has started to turn bright, the CI should research past performance in a similar time period to see which fund did the best in a bull market and invest money into that fund. When the market is not drastically changing, give the most substantial weight to a three-year time period, then five-year time period, and finally a one-year time period.

History demonstrates that the stock market often rotates between value and growth and between large capitalization stocks and small capitalization stocks. The three- and five-year averages will not only verify the manager's being in the correct sector during a market cycle, but it will inform the CI of what sectors are good investments. Also, the average bear market has lasted between nine and 18 months. A three-year track record will engulf the average bear market and give the investor an idea of how the fund will perform in bad times. When selecting a fund, it is always wise to go back and see how the fund performed in bad market conditions. For example: October 1987, October 1990 and October 2000 until July 2002. During the selection process, choose the top five funds in each class by giving more weight to the three- and five-year returns. Then narrow the search by picking the top two or three funds, based on how they did in the bad market conditions. This process will assist you in picking true winners.

Begin your quest by examining current one-year market winners. Then see which ones did well over a three- and five-year time period. Compare apples to apples. Never compare an aggressive growth fund to a balanced fund. Compare an aggressive fund to an aggressive fund, or a balanced fund to a balanced fund. This procedure quickly shows which fund performed the best in one-, three- and five-year time periods in their risk category. Some top performers in a one-year time period luckily have been in the right place at the right time. Luck, not skill, produces the returns. Looking at longer-term track records will reassure the investor that the performance was due to skill and not luck.

Securities Turnover

Securities turnover is the number of times securities were bought and sold within a portfolio during a certain period of time, usually a year. When screening for turnover, most CIs should look for funds with low portfolio turnover. High turnover can sometimes lead to tax inefficiency and embedded transaction cost, which can equate to lower after-tax returns. Turnover should not be a primary screen in the selection process; however, in comparing two comparable funds, other things being equal, you should choose the fund with the lowest portfolio turnover.

Fund Expenses

When considering fund expenses, lower is better. The annual expense ratio expresses the percentage of assets deducted each fiscal year for fund-operating expenses, including 12b-1 fees, management fees, administrative fees, operating costs, and all other asset-based costs, except brokerage costs, incurred by the fund. Sales charges on loaded funds are not included in the expense ratio. It is a mistake to excuse high expenses on mutual funds because they tend to drag the performance of a fund down over a long period of time. A good rule of thumb to use for stock funds is to look for funds that have an expense ratio below 1.90 percent. For fixed-income funds, look for funds with expense ratios below .90 percent.

Fund Size

Many academic studies have examined the correlation between the size of a fund and its performance. The universal conclusion has been that big is not necessarily wonderful. The largest mutual funds are rarely among the top performers in a bull market. Many large funds have excellent long-term track records although most were not large funds at the beginning when they were recording the bulk of their cumulative gains. The main advantage of smaller funds is that the fund has greater opportunity to realize the benefit of superior portfolio management by investing in smaller companies. A large fund cannot take a meaningful position in minuscule companies. Only a small amount of stock is available, and legal consideration will allow a company to own a limited amount of voting stock. In the cases of bond funds and money market mutual funds, larger is better because of a lower expense ratio.

Fund Family

Stockbrokers pushed fund family over the last 25 years because of the sales load the brokerage firm was charging the client. If you got tired of the fund, or your investment objectives changed, you could switch in the family of funds without paying another sales charge. When buying no-load funds, the fund family is not as important because you can switch fund families without paying a load. Large fund families have an advantage when it comes to a star fund manager leaving a fund. Typically the larger the fund family is, the less significant the departure of a star manager will make on the fund. It is easier for a larger fund family to replace a departing manager with someone equally skilled. A good example of this is when Peter Lynch left the Fidelity Magellan fund and they replaced him with another highly skilled fund manager.

Fund Manager

Know your fund manager. The prospectus is required to name the portfolio managers of a fund. The prospectus will give the fund manager's length of service and experience for the past five years. The number one reason to know your fund manager is in case he leaves the fund. Usually when a good performing fund switches managers,

The Selection Process

the funds performance tends to slump. The CI should do his or her homework and examine the fund to make sure that the long-term track record of the fund being analyzed was performed by the current fund manager. If not, the CI should avoid the fund. Committees manage some funds, so it is hard to tell who actually has the decision-making authority. Some committees have equal voice, while others have a team leader. In either case when a committee runs a mutual fund, the CI should not be concerned if one of its members leaves the committee. The Govett smaller companies' growth fund was ranked number 1 in 1993 and 1994, and number 2 in 1995. For 1996, Govett was ranked next to last, and in 1997 the fund was ranked fourth from last. What caused the big falloff in 1996 and 1997? Garret Van Wagoner, the mutual fund manager, left the fund in 1995. Just after his departure, the fund went south. The CI must know his or her mutual fund managers in order to guard against such circumstances.

It is crucial that the CI be a long-term investor. All other ways will lead to poverty. The Bible tells us in Proverbs 21:5: "The thoughts of the diligent tend only to plenteousness; but of every one that is hasty only to want." The long-term investing of the wise will increase in abundance, but those who look to get there quickly will not succeed.

God's will for the Christian investor is to obtain wealth, but we must do it God's way—the long-term investing way. If we went from poverty to wealth overnight, most individuals would not be able to handle such quick success, because it takes prudence to keep quick profits. *Prudence* has been defined as "wisdom in action, choosing the best means to an end." Proverbs 13:16 tells us that "every prudent man dealeth with knowledge." It takes wisdom and knowledge to obtain and keep wealth. It has been my experience that Christians and non-Christians who obtain wealth quickly do not keep it very long. They have not developed the knowledge needed to protect their assets. I had a high school friend who received a seven-figure settlement in a lawsuit. He took the settlement in a lump sum and in one and a half years he was completely broke. I know of many cases just like this. God's will is for us to obtain wealth, but He wants us to be able to handle the wealth.

Mutual Fund

For mutual funds the best source for information is *Morningstar Publications*. In *Illustration 4*, there is an example of the stock mutual funds buyer's worksheet. The worksheet lists several popular growth stocks and how the selection process works. In this illustration, notice the Berger 100 fund. The fund changed managers in year 2000. So, the newly selected fund manager was not responsible for the three- and five-year performance of the fund. Do not purchase such a fund.

The Berger 100 fund had a poor one- and three-year performance; however, even if the results were favorable, buying the fund would be inadvisable, because the fund manager was changed. Always give the manager two or three years to prove himself before considering the fund. In this illustration, the Federated Kaufman fund had the highest risk-adjusted performance (Sharpe ratio); however, the expense ratio for the fund is higher than our 1.90 percent expense ratio guideline. The Strong growth fund and the T. Rowe Price growth fund both came in with the same risk-adjusted performance. With a closer look, however, the CI would notice that the three-year track record of the Strong growth fund is 4 percent higher, but it is three times worse in a bear market (year 2000), which is the year for the one-year returns. The five-year annualized return, the T. Rowe Price outperformed the Strong growth fund by $3\frac{1}{2}$ percent. The beta for the T. Rowe Price fund is 1.05 versus 1.16 for the Strong. The T. Rowe price fund then has generated a greater five-year return with less risk. The wise CI would have chosen the T. Rowe Price growth fund out of this illustration for his growth fund of choice.

The Selection Process

EXAMPLE

Illustration 4

Bond Mutual Fund Buyer's Worksheet

Fund Name	Fund Category	Quote Symbol	Sharpe Ratio (Higher is better.)	Avg. Credit Quality	Total Assets (SM) (Lower is better.)	Manager in place since (Year)	Manager's Name	Annual Operating Expense Ratio (Lower is better.)	Total Returns Avg. 5yr.	Annualized 3yr.	Total Return 1yr.
CGM Capitol Dev	Growth	LOMCX	-.45	.98	422	1977	Heebner	1.08	4.91	-4.22	-17.77
Federated Kaufman	Growth	KAUFX	.23	.85	3B	1986	Utsch	1.94	11.26	13.35	6.23
Berger 100	Growth	BEONX	-.13	1.46	1B	2000	Tracey	1.13	7.18	1.23	-35.42
Fidelity Blue Chip	Growth	FBGRX	.07	1.09	24B	1996	McDowell	.86	14.62	7.29	-17.04
Gabeth Growth	Growth	GABGX	.20	1.23	3B	1995	Ward	1.37	18.75	10.55	-25.19
Harbor Growth	Growth	HAGWX	.18	1.48	166	1997	Welles	.88	12.67	15.91	-33.11
Strong Growth	Growth	SGROX	.21	1.16	2B	1993	Ogner	1.20	13.16	13.73	-31.61
T Rowe Price Growth	Growth	PRGFX	.21	1.05	5B	1997	Smith	.74	16.59	9.44	-9.46
White Oak Growth	Growth	WOGSX	.16	1.62	4B	1992	Oelschlager	.96	19.38	12.03	-32.2
Babson Growth	Growth	BABSX	-.11	1.16	354	1996	Gribbell	.79	12.27	3.45	-21.86
Tweedy Browne	Growth	TWEBX	.09	.51	977	1993	Browne	1.37	15.24	6.52	20.02
Amer. Cent. Ultra	Growth	TWCUX	.04	1.28	30B	1996	Wimbarly	.99	12.16	6.23	-23.64

Mission Possible

In *Illustration 5*, a look at a selection of bond mutual funds shows the Strong Corporate bond fund and the Janus Flexible bond fund. Both of the funds have the lowest credit quality of all the other bond funds listed. The lower the credit quality, the riskier the bond investment. The T. Rowe Price GNMA fund has a new manager, who did not generate the returns listed. The fund of choice in this illustration for the CI would be the Harbor bond fund. This fund has the highest three-year track record and a good credit quality of AA-rated bonds. In addition, duration is rather short, only 5.2 years. The annual expense ratio is below recommended maximum guidelines of .90 percent. The Harbor bond fund's five-year return is third, only behind the American Century Target 2010, which has almost double the duration, and the Strong Corporate bond fund (a much lower credit quality of bonds in its portfolio). The easy bond choice would be the Harbor bond fund.

Whatever the investment vehicle—stocks, bonds or mutual funds—there is a potential reward. Reaching that goal entails a certain degree of risk inherent in the investment vehicle. Always choose the investment that has the greatest amount of reward for the amount of risk taken. This sounds so elementary, but you should always study the returns versus the risk taken. Do not get caught up in just looking at returns.

All the research information needed in the selection process can be found on *Morningstar Publications*. Some local libraries carry *Morningstar*, or you can go on the Web to *www.morningstar.com* for this information. Use *Worksheet 2* (appendix, p. 146) and *3* (appendix, pg. 147) for your mutual fund selection process.

The Selection Process

EXAMPLE

Illustration 5

Stock Mutual Fund Buyer's Worksheet

Fund Name	Fund Category	Quote Symbol	Sharpe Ratio (Higher is better.)	Beta	Total Assets (SM) (Lower is better.)	Manager in place since (Year)	Manager's Name	Annual Operating Expense Ratio (Lower is better.)	Total Returns Avg. 5yr.	Annualized 3yr.	Total Return 1yr.
Jarius Short	Bond	JASBX	1.6	A	273	1996	Rufenacht	.65	6.84	6.15	9.49
Strong Short	Bond	SSTBX	1.9	A	1.2B	1990	Tank	.90	6.74	6.01	10.02
Schwab Tot BD	Bond	SWBDX	n/a	AA	307	1997	Daifotis	.35	6.53	6.36	10.52
Harbor Bond	Bond	HABDX	5.2	AA	904	1987	Gross	.60	8.12	6.69	10.88
Vanguard Short	Bond	VFSTX	2.2	A	6.6B	1982	MacKinnon	.25	6.79	6.42	10.35
Fidelity Inv. Grade	Bond	FBNDX	4.7	AA	3B	1997	Grant	.69	7.19	5.83	11.40
Fidelity Inter. Gov.	Bond	FSTGX	3.2	AAA	806	1998	Dudley	.63	6.93	6.20	11.06
T Rowe Price	Bond	PRGMX	3.4	AAA	1B	2000	Bavely	.71	7.38	6.10	11.33
Vanguard GNMA	Bond	VFIIX	3.0	AAA	13B	1994	Kaplan	.27	7.78	6.53	11.24
Janus Flex	Bond	JAFIX	4.0	BBB	1.1B	1997	Speaker	.79	7.27	4.12	8.61
Strong Corp.	Bond	STCBX	5.7	BBB	1.1B	1998	Schucking	.80	8.54	5.73	13.10
Amer. Cent. Target 2010	Bond	BTTNX	9.4	AAA	270	MGT	MGT	.59	9.73	5.95	15.13

Summary

1. Be sure the objectives of the funds you are considering meet your personal investment objectives.

2. Use the worksheets provided for mutual fund screens.

3. Review the fund's one-year, three-year and five-year track record, with more emphasis on three-year than five-year and the least emphasis on one-year.

4. See that the current portfolio manager is the same manager who produced the track record you reviewed.

5. Always review the expense ratio of the fund you are considering.

6. Always research whether the fund has grown considerably over the last three years.

7. Always look at portfolio turnover with the funds you are considering. Less is better.

8. Review the Sharpe ratio of the fund for risk-adjusted performance. The higher the ratio, the better.

9. Review the duration for your bond mutual funds. The lower the duration, the better.

10. Make sure the beta of the stock fund portfolio matches your risk tolerances.

11. In the selection process, review the growth funds expense ratio. Make sure it is below 1.90 percent.

12. In the selection process, review the bond funds expense ratio. Make sure it is below .90 percent.

6

Asset Allocation and Diversification

Investments fall into three general categories: stocks, bonds and cash equivalents. An asset allocation plan is where you have your investments divided into a model portfolio of stocks, bonds and cash. Over the past 10 years, my personal assets have been invested into good quality stocks or mutual funds, whether the market was timed or not.

Timing the market over a prolonged period of time is tricky. No one has developed a successful system for market timing. If they did, it would no longer work when the masses found out about it. Since no one has been successful at market timing, the strategy the CI should take is a long-term asset allocation strategy, which has had good returns, but not necessarily in any single week, month, quarter or year. Many money managers and investment advisers flip-flop on asset allocation. The strong bull markets during the past two decades would have made most investors believe that asset allocation is only for the weak-hearted, unlearned, novice investor.

Long-Term Growth

However, during the prolonged bear market of 2000, 2001 and

Mission Possible

2002 many sophisticated investors and investment advisers realized that asset allocation is advisable for long-term growth. Many investors, who did not allocate their assets in their portfolios, realized that most of the profits they made from 1998 to 2001 have diminished. Most investors who invested strictly in stocks over the past five or six years seem to outpace investors who allocated their investments in various investment groups and sectors. During the bear market of 2000 and 2001, these investors, who appear to be low-risk takers for using an asset allocation strategy, caught up with the investors who did not diversify their assets. Over the past 20 years, investors have not experienced as many bear markets as history says they should have (usually about two bear markets over each decade).

With the prolonged bull market of the '80s and '90s, many investors did not experience what a bear market can do to a portfolio's value in a short period of time. Since many of these investors have never experienced a severe bear market, they think the only way to be invested is 100 percent in stocks. Bear markets have a way of smacking investors with reality. To summarize, investors who allocated their assets, over the long haul, have had equal or greater returns with less risk.

This is what the CI should strive for. Many academic studies show that asset allocation is the key to investment results over a long period of time. The choice of asset classes has far more impact on results than any other investment decision. Basic allocations are among bonds, stocks and cash. Within each classification are various types of bonds, stocks and cash-like investment vehicles. The CI should be a big proponent of asset allocation in the sense that model portfolios have flexible guidelines for investments.

Flexible Guidelines

Model portfolios should be flexible enough to take advantage of trends in the market. If a new bull market is starting, a conservative

Asset Allocation and Diversification

investor should not stick to strict guidelines the typical model portfolio recommends. Your asset allocation plan should be flexible enough to take advantage of bull markets, especially new bull markets. The typical strict asset allocation plan would have a conservative growth investor, invested in 45 percent in stocks, 45 percent in bonds and 10 percent in cash at all times, with no variance from these strict guidelines.

A CI can stay conservative by having a plan that is a little more flexible. For instance, in a new bull market the conservative investors should move the assets they have in cash into stocks and have a portfolio that looks more like 55 percent in stocks and 45 percent in bonds. A flexible asset allocation plan will have the conservative investor taking a more aggressive stance, while maintaining a conservative portfolio during good market conditions.

On the other hand, a flexible asset allocation plan will allow the conservative investor to move assets out of stocks into cash during bad market conditions. So, during bad market conditions or during inflated markets, the conservative investors can take a more conservative stance by having a portfolio that looks more like 20 percent in stocks, 45 percent in bonds and 35 percent in cash.

The question the investor should be asking is, how do you know when the market is over- or under-valued? The simplest way to discern the value of the market is by looking at historical price to earnings ratios of the S&P 500. The Standard & Poors 500 price to earnings ratio has averaged about 15 over the past 75 years. Over this time period, when the S&P 500 P/E ratio gets over 23, the market tends to correct. So, the rule of thumb the CI can use is when the P/E ratio of the S&P 500 starts to creep above 23, a more conservative stance with their portfolio should be taken by moving some funds into cash.

As long as the S&P's P/E ratio is below 20, the CI should continue to be aggressive. There are a few exceptions to the rule. During slowing economic times, earnings will remain high while the stock market drops. The CI must always remember that the market is a leading indicator, which means the market will react to news about six to nine months before it happens. So, during an economic slowdown the price of stocks will often drop, while reported earnings remain high, which will look as if there is value in the market. However, earnings will follow the downturn and P/E ratios will be high.

Sometimes when the economy has been soft for a while, the market anticipates a rebound in the economy and the stock market turns up, as earnings remain poor. In this situation, the P/E ratio of stock will appear inflated. Typically, the earnings will start catching up with prices. During times like these, the CI should look at forward-looking P/E ratios of the Standard & Poors 500. This is what analysts expect in the next 12 months. If the P/E ratio shows value, start to position your portfolio accordingly. If the market is still over price, stay conservative. You can find the P/E ratio all over the Web. You can use *www.clearstation.com* as a source of information when you need to get the P/E ratio for the S&P 500.

Follow God's Word

Some investors are concerned with the effect the Enron debacle is having on individual investors. The national media has been reporting that some Enron employees lost their life savings with the collapse of the company. These employees invested the majority of their retirement-plan dollars into Enron common stock. The media has been successful in causing investors to be concerned with the accounting procedures some companies have embraced. It seems like Enron duped even some professional analysts. As late as September 2000, the majority of stock analysts had recommended Enron as a buy.

When professionals are fooled, individual investors are especially vulnerable. Do not panic. The answer is simple. Follow God's

Asset Allocation and Diversification

Word. Proverbs 15:27 tells us, "He that is greedy of gain troubleth his own house." First Timothy 3:3 tells us not to be greedy with filthy gain. God's Word, along with basic investing knowledge, tells you to diversify your holdings. Consider Abraham, whose riches were diversified among silver, gold and cattle (see Genesis 13:2). Job, the wealthiest man in the East, had his riches diversified among sheep, camels, oxen, donkeys and houses. Notice, both of these men had diversified investments. Follow their examples.

ERISA

Either Enron employees were ignorant of the concept of diversification, or they were full of greed. The federal government has the Employee Retirement Income Security Act (ERISA) to protect the employee. ERISA requires their employers to educate their employees on the basics in investing. These Enron employees should have been educated on the risk associated with not diversifying their retirement portfolio. So, it seems that the driving force behind such a catastrophic lost was greed. Before the collapse, Enron stock was moving up in price at a fast rate, and these employees decided to put all their retirement-plan dollars into their company stock. Investment textbooks teach against such a practice, and common sense also tells us not to put all our eggs in one basket. If these employees had followed the simple truths of the Bible, their retirement plans would still be intact.

Conventional wisdom will tell you to invest 100 percent of your assets in stocks, especially during bull markets. Note the parallel with what the Bible tells us about what conventional wisdom will do to the Christian: "Enter ye in at the strait gate: for wide is the gate, and broad is the way, that leadeth to destruction, and many there be which go in thereat: Because strait is the gate, and narrow is the way, which leadeth unto life, and few there be that find it" (Matthew 7:13, 14). Conventional wisdom will also tell you to go the way of the crowd; it is the easy way and everybody is doing it. What most investors do not realize is that many investment philosophies looked good during the last five years because the environment was conducive for it to work. Most investors can have good returns during bull markets. But can their returns hold up in bad markets? It is disastrous to invest all your assets in stocks. Typically, when the pundits advise investments in growth stocks, the CI should be actually investing in value stocks and vice versa.

Diversified Portfolio

To achieve victory, CIs often will have to travel a separate way than the average investor. The road the average stock and mutual fund investor takes ordinarily leads to mediocrity and defeat. They often buy when they should be selling and sell when they should be buying; or getting in the market when they should be getting out of the market, and getting out of the market when they should be getting in.

Charts 1, 2 and *3* provide examples of a flexible asset allocation investment theology. Believe in simple asset allocation and diversification among top stocks, bonds and cash. In a bear market, when stocks are not doing well, go into cash. History has proven many times that the stock market growth over time is so strong that CIs should invest for growth. They should invest in stocks, a small portion in bonds and cash equivalents. The road that leads to investment mediocrity is wide and many go there. Do not let yourself be drawn into this wide road, but invest your hard-earned money for growth. Most portfolios have too little diversification and too much risk. If CIs would adopt a simple mix of assets, they would be more likely to achieve their long-term investment goals. This type of asset allocation is justified when capital reaches an immense sum, when a new investor is learning the ropes of investing. Asset allocation is justified at all times.

Asset Allocation and Diversification

Chart 1
Aggressive Plan
Flexible Asset Allocation Plan

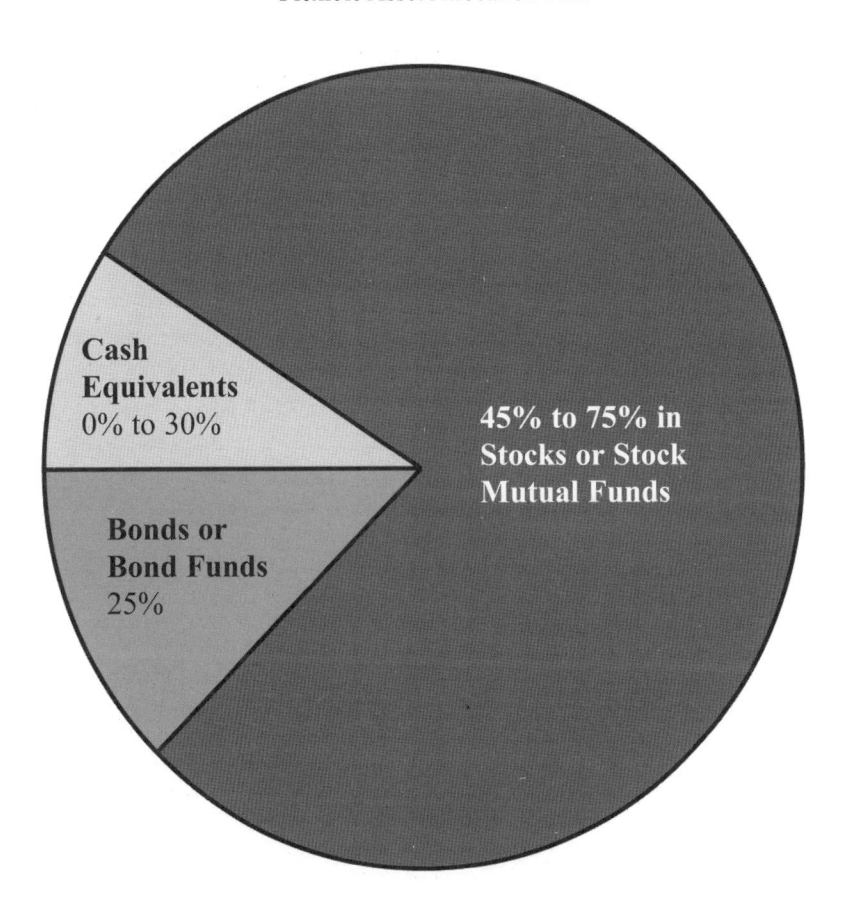

Cash Equivalents
0% to 30%

Bonds or Bond Funds
25%

45% to 75% in Stocks or Stock Mutual Funds

Bond percentages are to remain constant 25%, while percentages in stocks and stock mutual funds will be flexible depending on market conditions. Minimum in stocks should not fall below 45% with a maximum of 75% in stocks. Any amount not invested in stocks and bond or mutual funds should be invested in cash equivalents such as money market mutual funds.

Chart 2
Moderate Plan
Flexible Asset Allocation Plan

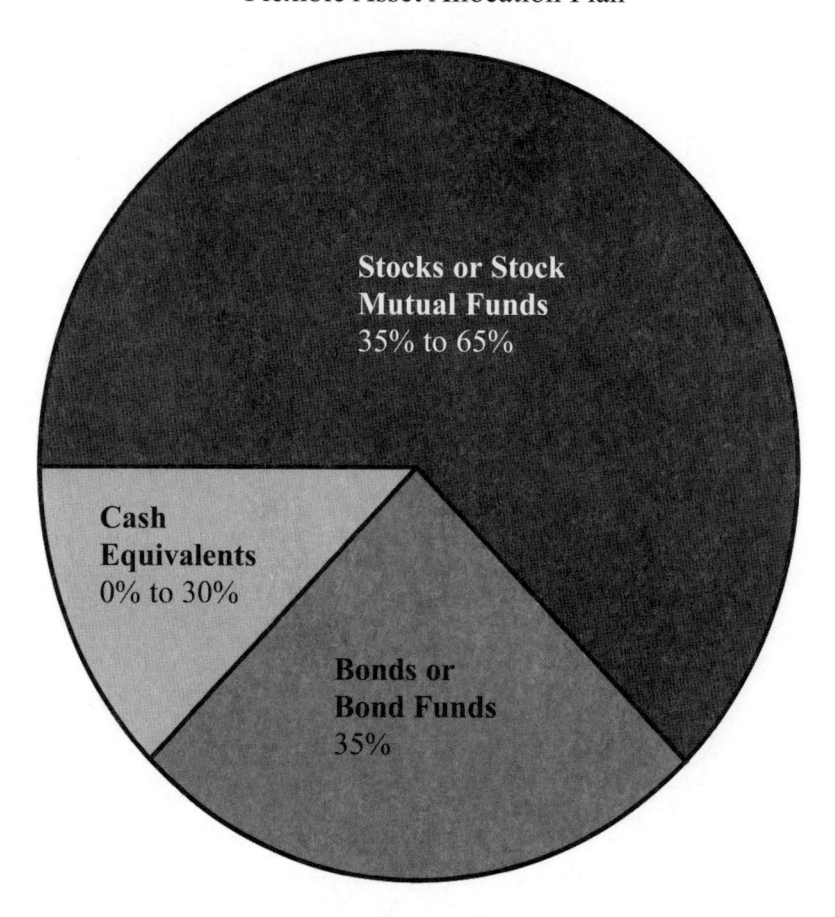

Stocks or Stock Mutual Funds
35% to 65%

Cash Equivalents
0% to 30%

Bonds or Bond Funds
35%

Bond percentages are to remain constant 35%, while percentages in stocks and stock mutual funds will be flexible depending on market conditions. Minimum in stocks should not fall below 35% with a maximum of 65% in stocks. Any amount not invested in stocks and bond or mutual funds should be invested in cash equivalents such as money market mutual funds.

Asset Allocation and Diversification

Chart 3
Aggressive Plan
Flexible Asset Allocation Plan

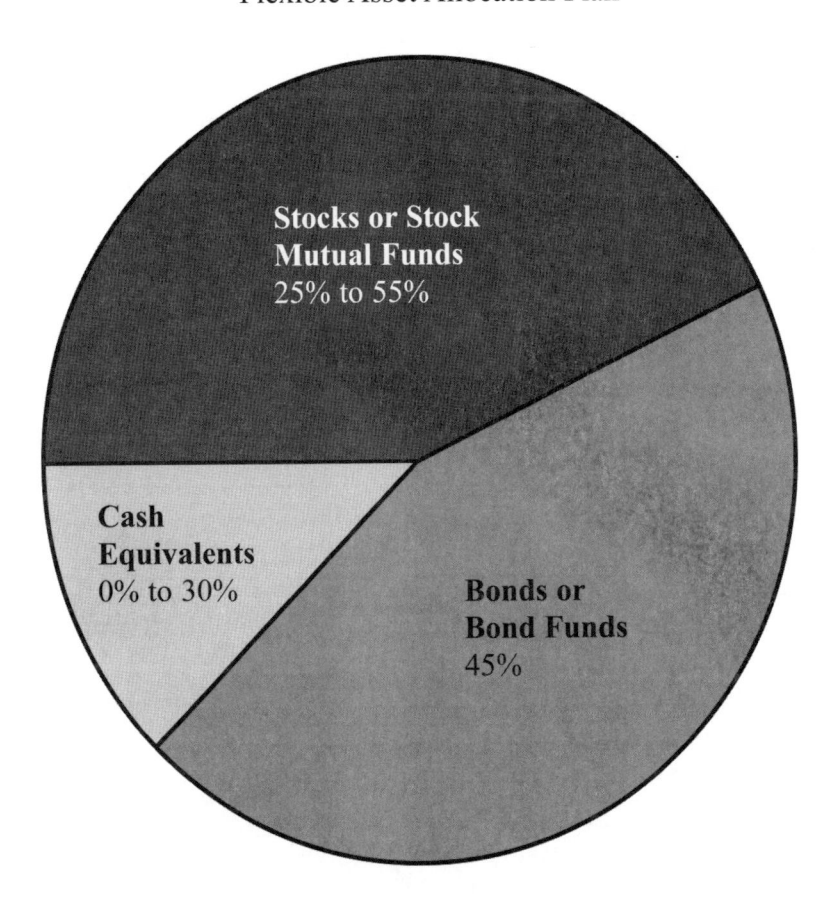

Stocks or Stock Mutual Funds
25% to 55%

Cash Equivalents
0% to 30%

Bonds or Bond Funds
45%

Bond percentages are to remain constant 45%, while percentages in stocks and stock mutual funds will be flexible depending on market conditions. Minimum in stocks should not fall below 25% with a maximum of 55% in stocks. Any amount not invested in stocks and bond or mutual funds should be invested in cash equivalents such as money market mutual funds.

Mission Possible

The CI investment objectives and risk tolerances will often, but not always, allow him or her to concentrate the investments for growth. What I mean by "concentrate the portfolio" is that the CI will invest his funds in a carefully selected portfolio of stock and mutual fund winners. I do not believe in putting all your eggs into one basket, but I do believe the growth-oriented CI can selectively purchase a portfolio of 15 or less stocks and a few bonds that can make them a substantial amount of money. A portfolio of 15 stocks can be well diversified among industries groups and individual stocks. Investing in only one stock is too risky. A portfolio of well-selected diversified stocks can catapult the CI into an accumulated wealth status.

The problem with most investors is that it is simply impossible to know all you need to know about a portfolio of 20 or more stocks. The CI does not have to own a score of stocks in order to achieve great success. When investing in mutual funds, the CI should never own more than eight mutual funds. Also, there is no need to purchase any more than three of any one sector when purchasing a mutual fund. By definition, mutual funds are somewhat diversified, so when you diversify more than eight funds, you tend to water down your total return per year.

Do not overdiversify. The selection of too many stocks or mutual funds is often a form of hedging against ignorance. Some investors believe it is safer; however, the chance for errors in judgment is greatly increased by overdiversification. Keeping up with too many stocks or mutual funds is very difficult. Concentrating on a few select stocks and not scattering your investment dollars will dramatically cut down on the amount of errors in judgment in the stock selection process. Your asset allocation strategy should be mostly concerned with allocating the equity (stock) piece of the pie. Though this book focuses chiefly on the growth aspect of investing, now is a good place to mention what the CI needs to know about investing in the bond portion of their portfolio. The main reason for including bonds in a portfolio is to provide stability and current income. The

Asset Allocation and Diversification

income is part of a portfolio's total return. Including more bonds in the portfolio will minimize growth and consequently the risk.

During poor market conditions the CI must take less risks. During good market conditions he or she should include more risk in the portfolio. Bonds vary dramatically. There are short, intermediate and long-term bonds. In general, longer bond maturities go together with higher yields and more risk. Then there is credit quality of bonds. The higher the credit quality, the safer the bond and typically the lower the yield. The CI who is investing for growth should have a diversified portfolio only with high-quality, investment-grade corporate or government bonds. High-quality investment-grade bonds are rated triple B or better by Standard & Poors.

Christian investments in individual bonds should include only A-rated or better bonds, because bond qualities change periodically based on the credit quality of the underlying company. You do not want to buy a BBB-rated bond. But later down the road the bonds credit quality gets dropped to junk status. United States Government bonds are rated AAA and the underlying credit quality has never been lowered. It has been my experience that bonds with maturities greater than five years are consistently not more rewarding, but more risky. Studies have shown that a five-year Treasury note annualized return has been equal to the 20-year Treasury bond with about half the risk. The best combination of individual bonds for stabilizing a stock portfolio is a laddered maturity date for bonds up to five years. An example of this would be if you need to invest $50,000 into bonds, balance your portfolio with the following mix:

$10,000 in one-year Treasury notes or corporate bonds
$10,000 in two-year Treasury notes or corporate bonds
$10,000 in three-year Treasury notes or corporate bonds
$10,000 in four-year Treasury notes or corporate bonds
$10,000 in five-year Treasury notes or corporate bonds
$50,000 grand total in bonds

When investing in bond mutual funds, buy only short-term bond

Mission Possible

funds to stabilize your investment portfolio. Since there are many short-term bond funds to choose from, make sure you check the average maturity date of the fund. The average maturity should be no longer than five years. Check the average credit quality of the short-term bond fund. The average credit quality should be an A or better rating by Standard & Poors.

These are the basic guidelines the CI should use when diversifying assets:

Equity Mutual Funds
$500 to $5,000 —————————— one or two funds
$5,000 to $25,000 —————————— one to four funds
$25,000 to $50,000 —————————— three to six funds
Over $50,000 —————— no more than eight funds

Short-Term Bond Funds
$500 to $5,000 —————————————— one fund
$5,000 to $25,000 —————————— one or two funds
$25,000 to $50,000 —————————— one to three funds
Over $50,00 —————— no more than four funds

Stocks
Less than $25,000, invest in mutual funds
$25,000 to $50,000 —————————— four to five stocks
$50,000 to $100,000 —————————— five to 10 stocks
$100,000 to $500,000 —————————— eight to 12 stocks
Over $500,000 —————————————— 10 to 15 stocks

Individual Bonds
Less than $25,000, invest in mutual funds
$25,000 to $50,000 —————————— one to two bonds
$50,000 to $100,000 —————————— two to three bonds
$100,000 to $500,000 —————————— three to four bonds
Over $500,000 —————————————— four to six bonds

Asset Allocation and Diversification

Summary

1. Mutual funds are a great way to handle diversification.
2. No more than eight equity mutual funds should be owned.
3. No more than three of any one sector of funds should be owned.
4. Your stock portfolio should have no more than 15 stocks.
5. Christian investors should invest for growth.
6. Christian investors should diversify among well-selected stocks or mutual funds.

7

Stock Section/ Fundamental Analysis

Some investors say, "I'll never be able to pick winning stocks." In fact, investing in winning stocks is not as difficult as the retail-brokerage industry would have you believe. Their success at convincing us is so great that Merrill Lynch, the largest retail brokerage firm in the United States, was a strong-performing stock over the last five years (33.5% a year), not far behind mighty Microsoft (34.5%), and ahead of Intel (25.6%) and Sun Microsystems (32.3%).

Depending on investable assets, a Christian's investment philosophy should invest in diversified individual stocks. This can be done with as little as $50,000. Investors with less than $50,000 should invest in growth mutual funds until their portfolio grows to the level of $50,000 before they start to invest in individual stocks. Purchasing individual stocks will make the CI higher investment returns if good stocks are chosen. A good comparison guide to follow in this action is the Standard & Poor's 500, a broadly based index of 500 companies to which growth domestic mutual funds are compared. The S&P 500 provided an annualized return of 14.41 percent over the last 10 years. For example, look at some of the

Mission Possible

best-known no-load fund families listed below with their best performing mutual funds over the latest 10-year period. All the funds listed below were superior to the S&P 500 over a 10-year period.

Family	Top Fund	10-Year Annualized Return (Data through 5/30/01)
INVESCO	Invesco Leisure	20.64%
VANGUARD	Vanguard Health Care	21.68%
T. ROWE PRICE	T. Rowe Price Science & Tech	17.71%
FIDELITY	Fidelity Select Electronics	28.78%
STRONG	Strong Advisor Common	17.98%
JANUS	Janus Growth & Income	19.13%

Notice that the best of these 10-year returns is with the Fidelity Select Electronics fund, which performed at 28.78 percent per year. Compare the returns of the top mutual funds with the returns of the top-ranked stocks. EMC Corp. returned 64.57 percent, Cisco Systems returned 57.35 percent, and Dell Computer returned 56.21 percent. Note the vast amount of difference here. The best of the three stocks listed is EMC Corp. averaging 64.57 percent per year, a little more than double the return of the Fidelity Select Electronics fund. However, dollarwise the difference is substantial. $10,000 in the Fidelity Select fund would have been worth a little more than $125,000. The same $10,000 in EMC Corp. would have been worth a little above $1.4 million. But the probability of successfully choosing the top stocks of all stocks might dissuade the CI. Do not worry. The probability is about the same as choosing the top-ranked mutual fund out of a database of 12,500 funds listed in the Morningstar database.

The mission looks to be impossible for the average CI. However, the following chapters will detail the picking of big winners in the stock market that have a minimum of mistakes. These techniques will show just how a February 1991 recommendation to my clients to purchase Cisco Systems returned nearly $1 million on a $10,000 investment.

Stock Section/Fundamental Analysis

Fundamental Analysis of Stocks

This is the starting point used in selecting the best common stocks. By definition, the fundamental approach to picking stocks is when an investor determines the value of a security by using information relating directly to the health of the firm and the economy. An analysis of the fundamentals of a company usually starts with a study of past earnings and an examination of company balance sheets. Fundamental analysis can give insight into future performance of the firm not yet recognized by the rest of the market. Serious application of the suggested approach will enable the long-term CI to structure a lifetime investment program with both security and capital appreciation.

All the CI's stock investments must be fundamentally sound, as is the CI's walk with the Lord. It is an issue of first things coming first: Be born again and make heaven your home, as stated in John 3:3. So, the first thing a Christian investor must do, to get to a point of accumulated wealth when investing in common stocks, is to stick with listed companies only. The stock should be listed on the NASDAQ, New York or American Stock exchanges. Other listed stocks with foreign stock exchanges are also acceptable.

The CI should avoid nonlisted companies because the risk/reward ratio typically is unfavorable. The Bible tells us that the two greatest commandments are to love God with all our hearts, minds, souls and strength and to love our neighbor as ourselves (Matthew 22:37, 39). These commandments are the sum of all divine revelation and responsibility. The two greatest fundamental analyses of stocks that Christians should look at are earnings growth and revenue growth.

Earnings

Earnings per share are calculated by dividing the earnings available to common shareholders by the average number of common shares outstanding. What the CI must know is that profit is the ultimate measure of success of a firm. Earnings growth always matters. It is the catalyst that drives up stock prices. In the late 1990s in the "dot com" boom, many analysts were saying earnings did not matter, because these dot com companies were breaking new ground in technology. The speculation was that these companies would generate a profit over the next three to five years. These stocks soared to unsustainable highs, because the companies were not making money. For example, Amazon's market capitalization (common stocks outstanding multiplied by market price of common stock) was equivalent to J.P. Morgan, but its earnings were only in the hundreds of thousands, while J.P. Morgan's earnings were in the hundreds of millions. Earnings always matter. In the bear market of 2000, Amazon's stock dropped substantially and J.P. Morgan's stock did not. When stocks get overvalued, many analysts and some money managers will sometimes say, "This time things are different."

Earnings always drive stock prices; things are the same. Without earnings, the only thing that can drive up a stock's price is hype. An inflated stock price cannot be substantiated with hype. Sound rational fundamental analysis is not a variable. Fundamentally, it is a simple truth. If a company is not making positive earnings, the price will eventually reflect the amount of earnings the company is making.

Stock Selection

During the stock selection process, the CI should compare the most recent reported earnings per share to the prior year's same quarter. The greater the percentage increase in earnings, the better the potential for capital gains. The growth of a company's earnings per share is the most important element in stock selection. What you must consider is that if the company's earnings are flat or headed down, there is no reason for the stock to appreciate in value.

Stock Section/Fundamental Analysis

In William O'Neil's book, *How to Make Money in Stocks,* his research shows most companies that are big winners have higher earnings growth in their most recently published quarter. Also, Christians should look for companies that show an increase in earnings on a yearly basis. The most recent reported earnings per share for the past four quarters should be higher than the prior four quarters. The CI needs to be wary of misleading reports about earnings made by a onetime extraordinary gain.

Nonrecurring profits will help make earnings per share growth look good, but it is a onetime extraordinary gain and not a continuous growth of earnings. The CI needs to look for the very best of companies that are consistently growing earnings the fastest. During the late 1980s, many companies were raiding their retirement plans for a onetime extraordinary capital gain. Many of these retirement accounts were overfunded, defined benefit plans. These companies put more money into their retirement plan than was needed. During the late '80s, the stock market crashed and many businesses slowed down, so the top management of many companies decided they would make earnings look better by raiding the employees' retirement plans. CIs must know if the earnings increase is a nonrecurring. If so, they should avoid purchasing these types of companies.

The CI should set a minimum guide for earnings growth to choose superior performing stocks. When selecting stocks, the minimum current earnings growth to look for is 25 percent. Look for a minimum of 20 percent yearly earnings growth. Many analysts will also forecast earnings for the next fiscal year. You can use a minimum of 30 percent current fiscal year earnings projections as a guide for selecting stocks. A company will have to meet all three guidelines before you should consider purchasing the stock. Current corporate earnings reports are available in the *Wall Street Journal* or *Investors Business Daily*. Many Web sites such as *CNBC.com, CBSmarketwatch.com,* and *msnmoneycentral.com* also have current corporate earnings reports.

CIs must have a positive outlook when investing. Many Christians and preachers subscribe to the "doom-and-gloom theory." They see with negative eyes. Attend to the Bible here: "Many are the afflictions of the righteous: but the Lord delivereth him out of them all" (Psalm 34:19).

Everything that we go through is just a test. Nothing more. James 1:1 tells us, "My brethren, count it all joy when ye fall into divers temptations."

Many investors love a good bull market; but the world-coming-to-an-end mentality takes over in a bear market. Just as the righteous suffer temptations, at times the investor will have to suffer a bear market. However, it is just a temporary test. The average bull market will last three to four years, while the average bear market will last only nine to 18 months. Do not be negative. Doing so makes it too easy to find a reason each year for not investing and getting the wealth accumulation process started.

The American funds group produced a poster dated from 1934 forward. Each year, reasons were given not to invest: 1934, the Depression; 1941, Pearl Harbor attack; 1947, Cold War with Russia. What the poster shows is that investors should not concern themselves with bad news. Positive, steady investing works. A single investment of $10,000 into the American ICA fund in 1934 would have been worth over $45 million in 1999, averaging over 13 percent annualized rate of return. Stay focused; stay positive.

Analyzing Earnings

Sales (revenue) growth is important when analyzing earnings per share growth. Companies reporting continuous high earnings per share growth without an adequate sales growth will eventually have a slowdown in earnings per share. For example, Coca Cola reported earnings per share growth of about 20 percent for many years. Without continuous sales growth, that would substantiate a high earning growth. Finally, in the late 1990s, earnings growth finally

Stock Section/Fundamental Analysis

suffered. Most companies cannot continue to show substantiated earnings growth without the sales growth to back it up. Above-average sales growth for a company is usually predicated on expected rapid growth of the industry in which it operates. For example, the personal computer industry has had substantial sales growth over the past 10 years. Likewise, Dell computer has had substantial sales growth over the past 10 years, along with Gateway and Compaq. The two most important fundamental ratios the CI should look for in purchasing stocks are earnings per share growth and revenue/sales growth. The two work hand in hand. The CI should look for the best companies with a minimum current quarter increase in earnings per share of 25 percent and a minimum annual earnings per share increase of 20 percent. Make sure these earnings are backed by an adequate increase in sales revenues. Otherwise, the earnings may not be substantiated in the near future. Look for companies with expected next-year earnings per share growth of a minimum of 30 percent.

The CI who wants to accumulate wealth should read the financial news pages, not the ones in your local newspaper—the *Wall Street Journal* or *Investors Business Daily*. Getting crucial financial data will be better served with a subscription to *Investors Business Daily* (*IBD*). The old saying "If you want to be rich, do what the affluent do" is true. The average net worth of the people who read *IBD* is $1.53 million and their average household income is $194,500. Their average value of their investment portfolio is $951,200.

In the stock tables of *IBD*, the first column ranks the earnings per share (EPS) of each stock. The rating measures the short- and long-term growth rate of the company. Results are compared to all other companies and are ranked from 1 to 99, with 99 being the best and 1 being the worst. A company that ranks 80 has earnings that outperformed 80 percent of all other companies. In other words, they are in the top 20 percent of all companies. The CI should not consider looking at a stock that has an EPS rank of less than 80. The ideal stock will be ranked in the top 20 percent of all companies in earnings growth.

Price-Earnings Ratio

Contrary to widespread opinion, the price-earnings ratio (P/E) is not an important rule in selecting stocks. The P/E ratio is simply the price of the stock divided by the earnings per share. P/E ratios have been used for years to determine if a stock is overvalued or undervalued based on the historical range of the P/E for a stock. Some investors would not consider purchasing any stock that had a P/E over 20. This is faulty thinking. Researching the history of superior performing stocks will show that superior performing stocks usually have a higher P/E ratios than the stock market average. Investing in stocks with a higher P/E ratio than the market average can result in missing all three of the better performing stocks over the past 10 years (EMC Corp., Cisco and Dell).

Some value-style portfolio managers will use a low P/E ratio philosophy when purchasing stocks. For example, they look for stocks whose P/E ratios fall among the lowest 40 percent of all stocks at any given moment in time. The period of time when P/E ratios are important is when the stock market is overpriced. It is foolish to purchase a stock that is selling at a P/E ratio so high it would be impossible for the company to live up to the expectations of such a P/E multiple.

During the dot com mania, companies such as Qualcom were selling at a P/E multiple of greater than 800 times earnings, as compared to about 23 times earnings on the Standard & Poors 500 index of stocks. When companies get this overvalued, the P/E ratio does matter. A company with a high P/E ratio must have incredible earnings growth to justify the high price placed on the stock. P/E ratios are lower on slow-growing stocks and higher on fast-growing stocks. The CI should not compare stocks in different industry groups, like comparing apples to oranges. The average P/E of Southern Company, an electric utility, should not be compared to

IBM. What is a bargain P/E ratio for IBM may not be a bargain for Southern Company. When purchasing stocks, do not pay more than four or five times more than what the average price-earnings ratio is on the Standard & Poors 500 index. The most important thing to remember about P/E ratios is to avoid stocks that have extremely high P/Es.

Financial Leverage

CIs should be interested in the amount of debt a company is carrying, because debt influences the rate of return and the amount of risk the CIs can expect to realize on their investment. Whenever a firm finances a portion of assets with debt, the firm is said to be using financial leverage. A banker will ask for a net worth statement when a borrower seeks to take out a loan. The net worth statement will include all assets minus all liabilities (debt). If the debt ratio is too high, the bank will not make the loan. Christians should look at a company's balance sheet to determine its debt load. Like the bank, if the debt is high, Christians should avoid investing in these stocks. Debt is broken down into current liabilities and long-term debt. Current liabilities are obligations that must be paid within one year, and long-term debt usually has a maturity of one to eight years. The CI can use several ratios to measure the degree to which a company is employing financial leverage. However, the one that the Christian investor needs to be familiarized with is the debt-to-equity ratio, which measures the financial strength of the company. This ratio is defined as follows:

$$\text{Debt-to-equity} = \frac{\text{Total Debt}}{\text{Stockholders' Equity}}$$

Stockholders' equity is sometimes called the book value of a firm. Some publications, like *Value Line,* will not give you the stockholders' equity, but they will state book value per share. To compute stockholders' equity, you must multiply book value per share by the number of common shares outstanding. A normal debt to equity ratio is around .33 or 33 percent. There is no magic number the CI should look for in analyzing the debt-to-equity ratio for a company, because the average debt-to-equity ratio varies among industry groups. What is high for one group might be low for another group. Find out if the debt-to-equity ratio for a company being analyzed is a good number; compare the number to at least three or four other companies in the same industry group. Common sense will tell you, however, when a company has a debt-to-equity ratio less than the normal debt-to-equity ratio of 33 percent. Debt should not be a problem for the company.

Value Line

The next item that needs consideration is the company. Certain questions need to be answered:
1. Your personal experience with the company
2. The quality and distinguishing aspects of the company's products and services
3. Managements potential and expertise in growing the company.

A domestic example here is useful. My wife loves to go to Michael's Arts and Crafts Store. The times I have gone with her, I noticed that the store is filled with women. She loves the layout of the store and the employees are helpful in answering questions. The store has everything she is looking for when she is making crafts for the church, plus interesting ideas for the creative woman. Likewise, I think we have a fixed expense and its name is Wal-Mart. My wife thinks she cannot go shopping unless she can visit Wal-Mart. I personally love to go to Home Depot. They have products that make even a righteous man covet. I love the lawn equipment and tools. The gist of this illustration is that if you like a company, it is likely other people do too. And if other people like it, maybe it is a possible candidate for a buy in your portfolio.

The best source for detailed financial histories of companies is in the *Value Line Investment Survey*, a comprehensive source of

Stock Section/Fundamental Analysis

information the CI can use to evaluate companies. *Value Line* has a rating and reports section on approximately 1,700 companies. Each report contains *Value Line's* "Industry Timeliness" report, which compares stocks for the best and worst buys over the next six to 12 months. A rank of 1 is their best buy and a rank of 5 is their worst buy. Also covered in the report is a safety ranking—a stock's forecast for the next three to five years and commentary on the stock.

Value Line is continually updating earnings estimates for the current year. Most of the time they give a yearly earnings forecast. Warren Buffett, the chairman of Berkshire Hathaway, said the following about *Value Line Investment Survey* in his 1998 annual meeting: "I don't know of any other system that's as good. . . . The snapshot it presents is an enormously effective way for us to garner information about various businesses. . . . I have yet to see a better way, including fooling around on the Internet, that gives me the information as quickly."

Peter Lynch supports Buffett in *One Up on Wall Street*: "*Value Line* is . . . the next best thing to having your own private securities analyst." The great thing about *Value Line* is that it can usually be found in the local library. If not, they can order it. Some investors who use *Value Line* and only look at the timeliness rank miss the other necessary information needed to purchase stocks. They purchase only the stocks that have a timeliness grade of 1. This is a faulty investing technique, because usually by the time the investor receives the update, the stock will have already moved up in price. Do not get caught up in buying a stock just because *Value Line* has the stock ranked as 1. Do your homework by looking for stocks that have a great line of products or services, and make sure the companies' earnings have grown by the recommended minimum. Use *Worksheet 5* (appendix, pg. 153) when you are analyzing stocks.

Computer Programs

Finally, computer access is a quick way to gather the fundamental

Mission Possible

information. Buy a copy of the software Telescan Investor's Platform with Prosearch, a sophisticated stock-screening system. Prosearch can look for stocks according to over 200 criteria including beta, price-earnings ratio and gross profit. The program can also search for mutual funds using more than 80 similar criteria. This program sells for about $400, plus about $67.95 per month for company reports and unlimited Prosearch screening. If the CI desires limited Prosearch screenings, the monthly price is considerably less. The personal computer revolution of the past 20 years has shattered the barrier between Wall Street and Main Street. It seems normal now, but just a few years ago Wall Street had a lock on the information individual investors needed to make informed decisions about buying stocks. With the personal computer revolution and explosion of software companies specializing in investment software, the individual investor now has access to all the much-needed information that is necessary to make sound investment decisions.

Take a look at *Illustration 6*. Listed are 14 stocks that meet all our minimum earnings per share growth criteria. Some of these companies have zero debt and some of them are fairly debt-leveraged. All 14 are ranked in the top 11 percent in earnings per share rank of those on the New York, American and NASDAQ markets. If any of these stocks were to have a timeliness rank of 4 or 5, they would not be a buy candidate. In your search, look for timeliness ranks of 1 or 2, a timeliness rank of 3 is questionable. However, if all other fundamentals on the company are strong, consider a 3.

Illustration 6
Fundamental Analysis Worksheet

Company Name	Stock Symbol	Stock Price	P/E Ratio	Debt to Equity Ratio	EPS Rank >80	Min. annual EPS growth >20%	Min. prior Qtr. EPS growth >25%	Min. projected next year EPS growth >30%	Timeliness Rank

Erratum
(page 96)

The chart at the bottom of the page (Illustration 6) is incomplete. It should appear as follows:

Illustration 6
Fundamental Analysis Worksheet

Company Name	Stock Symbol	Stock Price	P/E Ratio	Debt to Equity Ratio	EPS Rank >80	Min. annual EPS growth >20%	Min. prior Qtr. EPS growth >25%	Min. projected next year EPS growth >30%	Timeliness Rank
Ebay	EBAY	60.4	195.1	2.2	98	520	200	114.3	1
Wash Mut.	WM	38.4	14.8	N/A	96	20	40	36.5	2
Global Marine	GLM	16.5	21.5	69.9	93	116.2	228.5	113.8	3
KLA-Tencor	KLAC	49.8	23.2	0	94	108	26.3	42.4	2
Oakley	OO	12.2	27	25.3	96	132.3	62.5	34.2	3
Nabors	NBR	27.8	15.8	91.7	93	357.8	293.7	179	3
Lennar	LEN	46.5	9.6	107.8	98	71.2	118.7	44.8	1
PeopleSoft	PSFT	36	57	4.3	92	530	150	99.3	2
PayChex	PAYX	39.9	57	0	97	36	28.5	32.1	3
BOEING	BA	53.8	15.5	72.8	89	36.9	202	31.5	3
BJ Services	BJS	24.2	19.7	12.9	94	452.1	166.6	163.8	2
Forest Labs	FRX	73.9	62.8	0	99	84.3	137.5	41	2
Calpine	CPN	30	18.9	284.3	99	152.5	60	77.5	2
Ivax	IVX	36.4	44.1	41.6	98	100	107.1	51.3	1

Stock Section/Fundamental Analysis

Summary

1. Buy only listed stocks on the NYSE, ASE or NASDAQ.
2. Buy only stocks with the following minimums:
   a. Current quarter increase in earnings per share of 25 percent
   b. Annual increase in earnings per share of 20 percent
   c. Forecast for next year's earnings per share of 30 percent
3. Review earnings to assure earnings growth does not come from nonrecurring profits.
4. Review sales to make sure they are increasing with earnings.
5. Read the financial papers—*Investors Business Daily* and the *Wall Street Journal*.
6. Make sure the stock has a minimum EPS rank of 80.
7. Review a stock's P/E ratio. If it is more than five times the P/E ratio of the market, do not buy.
8. Review the stocks' long- and short-term debt.
9. Consider for purchase only these stocks with a *Value Line* timeliness rank of 1, 2 or 3.

8

Technical Analysis/ Reading Charts

Technical analysis is essentially the search for recurrent and predictable patterns in stock prices. Martin J. Pring defines it in his book Technical Analysis Explained as "a reflection of the idea that prices move in trends, which are determined by the changing attitudes of investors toward a variety of economic, monetary, political and psychological forces. The art of technical analysis—for it is an art—is to identify trend changes at an early stage and to maintain an investment posture until the weight of the evidence indicates that the trend has reversed." (p. 2) The wisdom of Solomon applies here. Proverbs 4:5, 6 says, "Get wisdom, get understanding: forget it not; neither decline from the words of my mouth. Forsake her not, and she shall preserve thee: love her, and she shall keep thee." Knowing how to apply technical analysis to the stock selection process will ensure a prosperous future.

Many times individuals will proclaim to be a Christian, but the fruit of the Spirit is not manifested in their lives. Likewise, a stock will look like a good stock, but technically the good fruit is not there. Matthew 7:17 tells us, "Every good tree bringeth forth good fruit; but a corrupt tree bringeth forth evil fruit." A good tree cannot

Mission Possible

produce bad fruit, neither can a bad tree produce good fruit. CIs are looking for the very best stocks that manufacture the very best fruits. The CI should look for stocks that have the potential to produce the highest annual returns for them. The Bible tells us to mark that perfect man. Fundamentally and technically, Job was perfect before God. Job did everything right. Jesus said this about Nathanael, one of the 12 apostles: "Behold, an Israelite indeed, in whom is no deceit" (John 1:47, *NKJV*). CIs should apply this principle when they are selecting stocks for their portfolio. Only the very best will do. We do not want to be deceived by a stock that only looks good—it must also perform well. Apply both fundamental and technical analyses in your stock selection process.

Reading Charts

In this chapter, CIs are going to learn the basics in reading charts of past stock prices and learn patterns they can exploit to make big profits in the stock market. Just like a physician uses CAT scans, X-rays and EKGs to know what is going on inside the body, the CI should learn to read charts to diagnose what is going on with a stock. A physician or nurse would not dream of giving a patient health care service without first looking at the patient's chart or past medical records. If they did, they would open the door for a flood of major malpractice lawsuits.

A CI who does not look and study stock charts is guilty of malpractice. Chart books such as R.W. Mansfield's allows the study of a large quantity of stock graphs in an organized manner. Many computer stock programs such as Telescan Investors Platform will chart stocks as the price changes during market hours. Some Web sites such as *CNBC.com* and *CBS.Marketwatch.com* also offer charts for analysis. Experience shows that investors who use only fundamental analyses in their stock selection will not experience superior investment returns. Neither will investors who use only technical analysis in their stock selection experience above-average

Technical Analysis/Reading Charts

returns. In spite of that, the combination of using fundamental and technical analysis together in your stock selection greatly increases your odds in selecting superior performing stocks.

Again it is a case of a recurrent historical Biblical moment. When the children of Israel were blessed of God, they could handle the blessing and peace only for about one generation before they fell into sin. Israel then would repent and call upon the Lord their God. God would answer their prayer with restoration and blessings. This became a vicious cycle. History also repeats itself in the stock market. Christian investors can use patterns of past stock winners to pick new stock winners.

In the stock selection process, the use of stock charts is critical. Fundamental analysis will help the investor pick the very best stocks, and technical analysis (charting) determines when they are favorably priced. Many investors will use fundamental analysis when buying stocks. Even fewer investors use technical analysis in their endeavors to purchase stocks.

Many Christians struggle to live for God and never can seem to get the closeness with God they desire. These Christians go to church on a regular basis and try to live above reproach. However, one of the main ingredients for living close to God is often omitted. These ingredients are prayer, reading and studying the Bible. They do only part of what is needed to walk with God. But the Bible teaches that we must study to show ourselves approved (2 Timothy 2:15). Approved of what? Approved to receive all that God has promised. If CIs are going to be successful in the stock selection process, they must add to the process the studying of charts patterns.

The Trading Range

Most all chart patterns in technical analysis show how price movements are related to breakouts around resistance or support levels. A resistance level is where selling pressures are expected to appear. A support level is where substantial buying is expected to

Mission Possible

appear. When a stock is moving between the support and resistance level, it is called the "trading range."

Look at the chart of the Dow Jones 30 Industrial Average. The long-term trading range is between 9,600 and 11,600 with major resistance at 11,600 and major support around 9,600.

The CI must know about support levels and that a stock purchase should be as close to the support level as possible. If the stock goes below its support level, there are negative implications for the stock. Most of the time, it will go considerably lower. The CI should try to buy a stock within 5 percent and no more than 10 percent above its support level. When stock trades close to its support level for a long period of time and finally penetrates the support level, a negative signal is given. The stock should not be purchased until it forms a new trading range. Once again, the purchase price should be within 10 percent of its new support level.

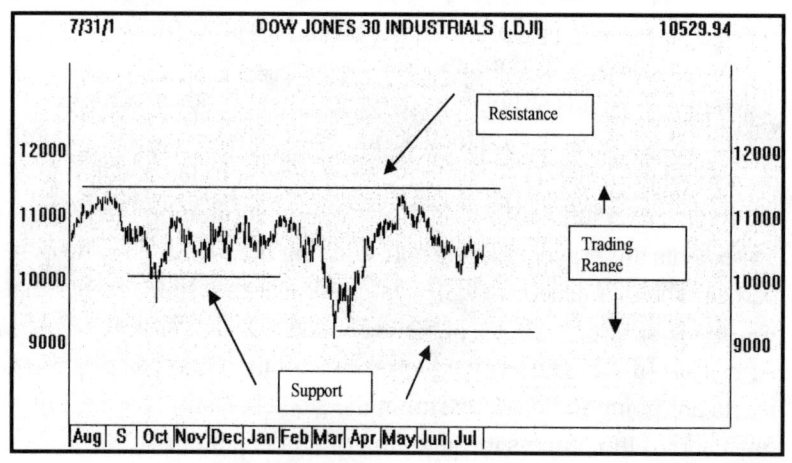

As the big decline takes place, as in the bear market of 2000, new support levels will form. Take a closer look at the same chart of the Dow Jones 30 Industrials. The chart shows how the support and resistance levels changed as the index went down. Also remember the support and resistance levels will go up as a stock increases in value.

Technical Analysis/Reading Charts

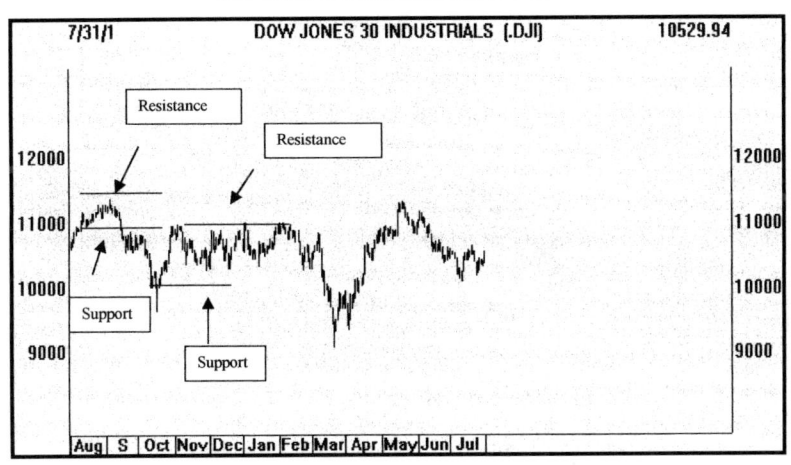

[Chart: DOW JONES 30 INDUSTRIALS (.DJI), 7/31/1, 10529.94, showing Resistance and Support levels from Aug through Jul]

Just like with the support level, the more times the resistance level is tested, and the longer the time period involved, the more bullish (positive) the signal. Stocks that overcome their resistance levels and make a new all-time high signify a bullish stock.

A stock that breaks out above its resistance level then becomes the new support level. Also, when a stock penetrates below the support level, the old support level becomes the new resistance level. Notice in the previous chart how the Dow Jones 30 Industrials penetrated below the support line in October and the old support line became the new resistance level.

The Moving Average

The CI should know how to use a stock's moving average. The moving average (MA) will alert the investor when a stock is about to make a short- and long-term move. A *moving average* is the average price of the stock over a designated time. In technical analysis, this is plotted on a chart. It is called a moving average because the price changes as the price of the stock changes or moves across a chart. The two most common long-term moving averages are the 200-day and the 30-week (also called 150-day moving average). The 10-week moving average (short-term) is more often used by traders. Which of the two long-term moving averages to use often depends

Mission Possible

on which one is initially comfortable. The 200-day is just a little longer-term average than the 30-week.

When using moving averages, stocks that are trading below their 30-week moving average should be avoided. The best time to buy a stock is when it has broken out of its resistance level and is moving higher in price. Another positive sign is when the 10-week moving average crosses over the 30-week moving average as the stock is moving up in price.

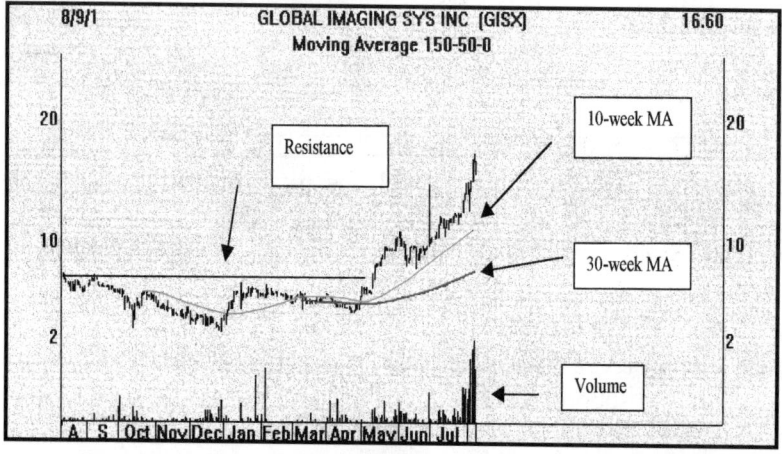

Look at the chart of Global Imaging. The 10-week moving average crossed over the the 30-week moving average in May 2001. If the the CIs would have drawn their resistance level lines, they would have noticed the stock broke out of its resistance level also in May. This is a very positive technical sign. If the CI had purchased the stock in May of 2001, in less than three months the CI could have doubled the investment.

Nearly all true breakouts will show a dramatic increase in daily trading volume. Look for trading volumes of at least one and one-half times the average daily trading volume when a stock breaks out its trading range. It is very important for volume to be larger than normal on a breakout. On many occasions, if a stock does not have a substantial increase in volume, the breakout is false and the stock will

Technical Analysis/Reading Charts

pull back and trade back into its normal trading range. The analysis of a stocks volume (number of shares being traded) will surely help the CI recognize if a stock is under accumulation (buying pressure) or distribution (selling pressure). It is a favorable signal when volume expands as a stock is rising in price and decreases as a stock falls in price. If a stock is moving upward with a increase in daily volume, the stock is being accumulated. Also, if the stock has normal or high daily volume and is going down, the stock is under distribution. The CI should buy stocks that are in the accumulation phase. *Investors Business Daily* offers a ranking on each stock from A to E, with A being a stock under heavy accumulation and E a stock under heavy distribution. The CI should only buy a stock that ranks C or higher. More emphasis should be placed on stocks ranked A or B.

Trend Lines

Most all stocks move in trends. When a stock chart is reviewed, a trend will be noticed: either up, down or consolidating. A trend line can be drawn on a chart to help the investor visualize the trend. Draw a trend line to connect at least two lows (a series of bottoms), or two highs (a series of tops), and there it is. Earlier reference to support and resistance levels are depicted in the example of the trend lines drawn on Compaq Computer Corp.

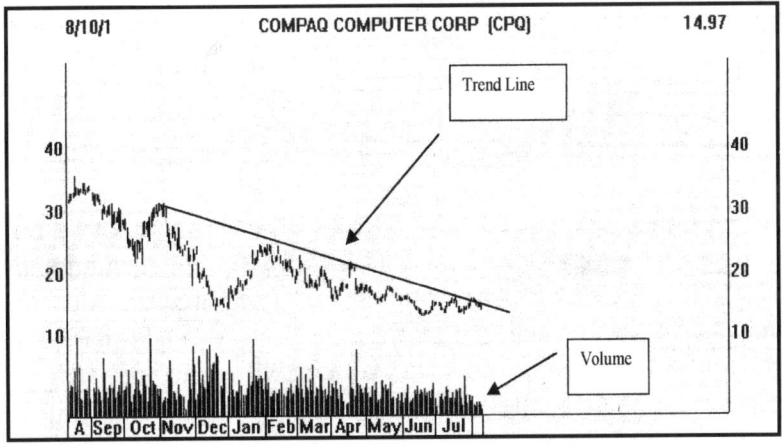

Mission Possible

Notice how the trend line is touched four times—once in November, once in April and twice in July. At the time this chart was drawn, Compaq was still in a downward trend. The CI who was looking to purchase Compaq would not purchase this stock until the stock had an upward trend. In the next chart on Cooper, the trend line is upward. If the stock were to trade below the trend line, it would be a possible sell signal. Trend lines are essential in determining when a trend has reversed. So, there are two possibilities that can happen when a trend line is penetrated. The stock will either have a trend reversal or a slowing down in the pace of the trend.

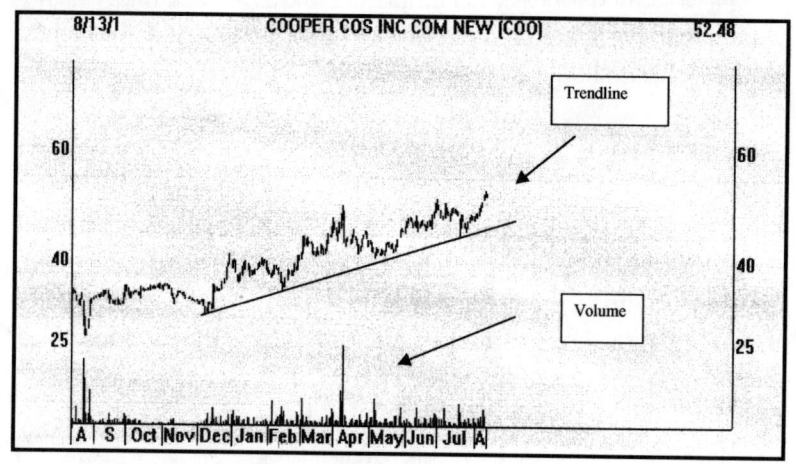

The Basing Structure

A wonderful price pattern to look for when analyzing a chart is to look for reliable base structures that have a minimum of six to eight weeks of price consolidation. The longer the base structure before a breakout, the better. Stock that has been either moving up or down for several months will eventually lose momentum and start to trend sideways. This motion is the basing structure. Most of the time, the volume will dry up as a base forms. When the base has been in existence for a while, the volume will sometimes start to expand, even though the price on the stock remains unchanged.

Technical Analysis/Reading Charts

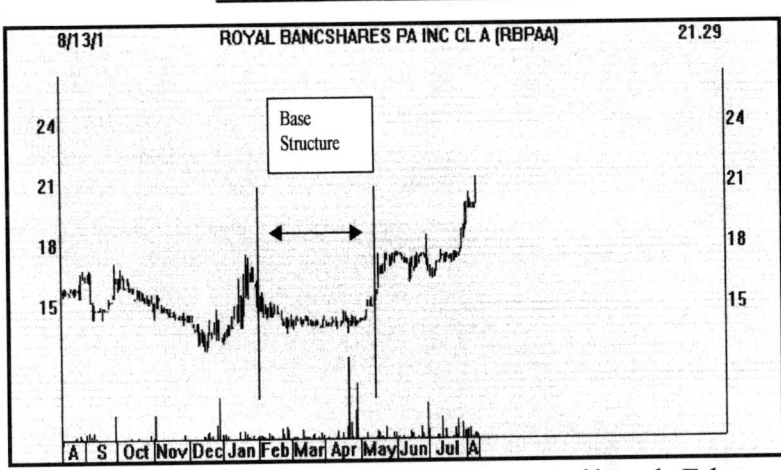

The basing structure on Royal Bancshares started in early February and lasted until mid-May before the stock started its upward advance. The CI should closely observe a company that is in a tight basing structure and wait until it advances out of the basing structure before the stock is considered for purchase. If you have a chart of a stock that has corrected and is in the midst of forming a base structure, make sure the base structure is more than six weeks old. If it is less than six weeks old, often the stock has not spent enough time at the bottom. Stocks with bases of less than six weeks old should be avoided.

Other Patterns

A "cup-with-a handle" price pattern is often the starting point of a stock that makes a lucrative price run. The chart looks like a cup with a handle when viewed from the side. A cup pattern usually lasts between three to six months, but the typical handle pattern will last between one and seven weeks. Though a handle should have a downward price drift, many times it does not. On the next move up it often stalls. Just make sure the handle price is above the stock's 30-week moving average. Handles that are below the 30-week moving average will often fail. View the cup-with-a-handle price pattern of Barr Laboratories.

Mission Possible

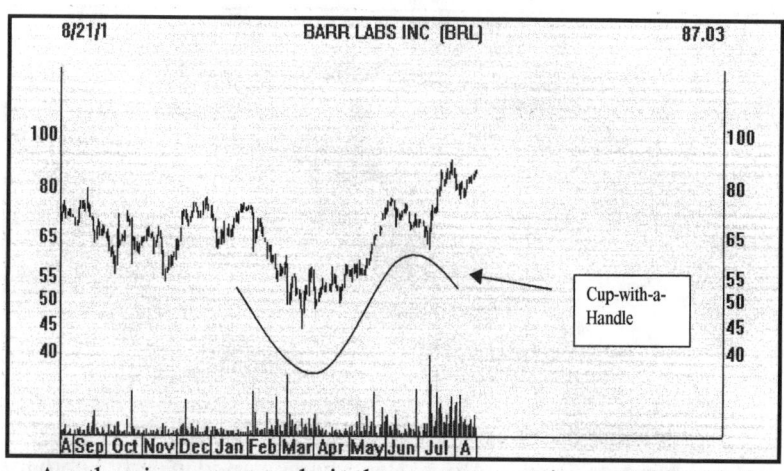

Chart: BARR LABS INC (BRL) 8/21/1 — 87.03, showing Cup-with-a-Handle pattern, with price scale 40–100 and months Sep through Aug.

Another important technical measurement is a stock's relative price performance. A one-year relative price performance is computed by taking the stock's current price multiplied by 100 and then divided by the price of one year ago. This number will tell you how the stock behaved in the market over the past 12 months. IBD measures the relative price performance compared to all other stocks. They call this their relative price strength rating (RS). The relative strengths are ranked from 1 to 99 (99 being the best, 1 being the worst). The relative strength will let you know the momentum of a stock. Isaac Newton's first law of motion says, "What is motion will stay in motion." So if you have a stock that is in the top of the RS ranking, the thought would be that it should continue being a winner and not a laggard. The problem with stating a minimum RS rank is that during a bear market, you will miss many good quality growth stocks on their upward move before the RS rank gets to where you can purchase the stock. During a confirmed bull market, the CI should not purchase a stock with a relative price strength of less than 75.

Some charting services, such as Mansfields, will plot a relative strength line. Unlike the RS rating which is a 12-month numerical rating, an RS line on a chart will plot the stock's strength versus the

Technical Analysis/Reading Charts

Standard & Poor's 500. So, when the line is moving up, the stock is outperforming the S&P, and when the line is falling, the stock is lagging the S&P. If the relative strength line is in a downward trend, do not consider buying the stock even if it breaks out above its resistance line.

The next exciting concept to move on to is in the next chapter, "When to Sell." First, here is a quick "prep" quiz on the basics in technical analysis.

1. Analyze these stock charts and draw support and resistance levels for each chart.

2. Draw a trend line for each chart.

3. Decide where the best one or two places to purchase these stocks would be.

4. Study these charts' agreement with the answers on their support and resistance levels, trend lines and best purchase price is the purpose of this exercise. Learning to read charts will assist you in selecting superior performing stocks. The answers follow the charts.

Quiz

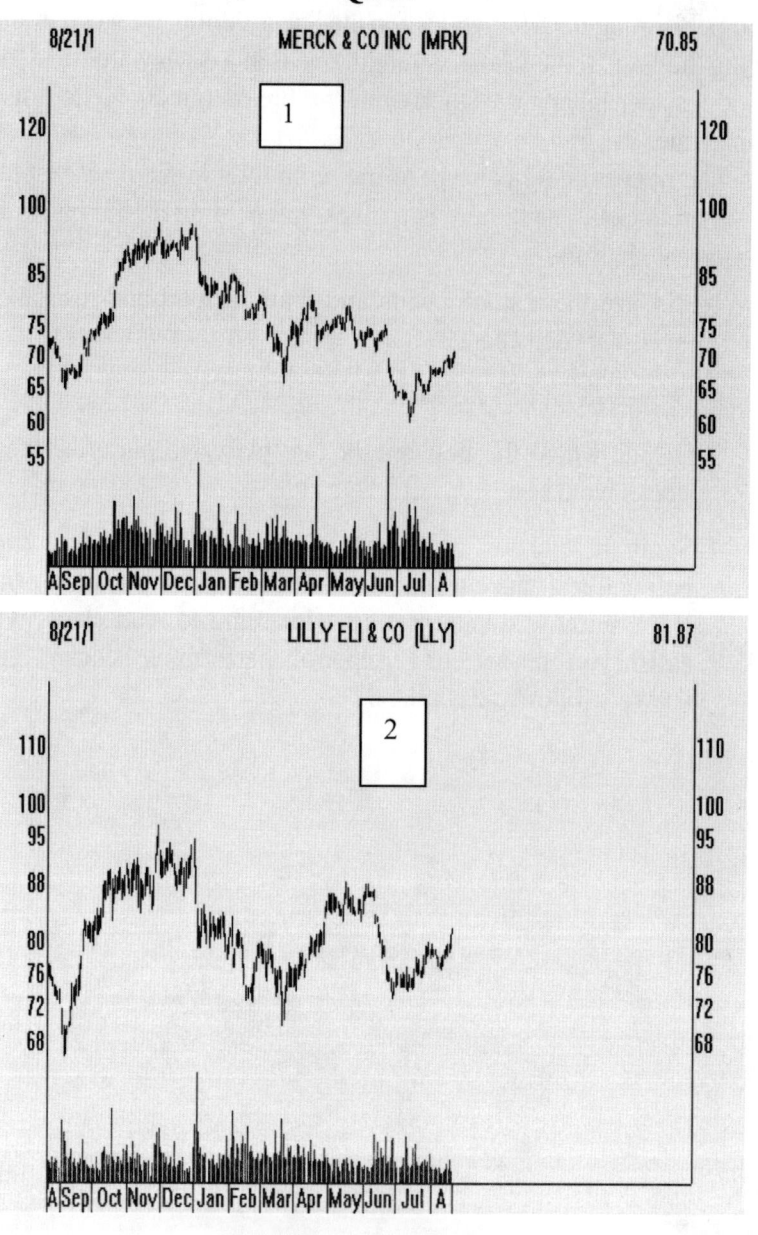

| 8/21/1 | MERCK & CO INC (MRK) | 70.85 |

[1]

| 8/21/1 | LILLY ELI & CO (LLY) | 81.87 |

[2]

Technical Analysis/Reading Charts

Quiz (cont.)

| 8/21/1 | ALPHARMA INC CL A (ALO) | 29.66 |

3

| 8/21/1 | ROBERT HALF INTL INC (RHI) | 27.05 |

4

Mission Possible

Quiz (cont.)

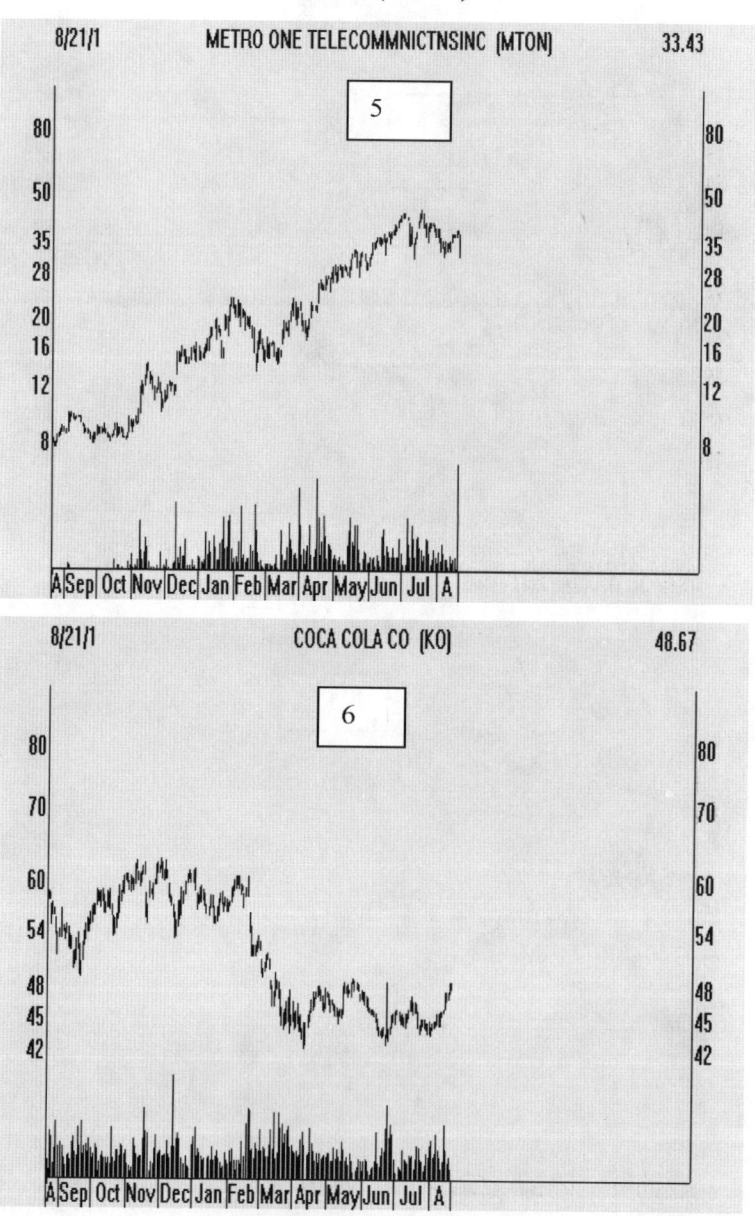

8/21/1   METRO ONE TELECOMMNICTNSINC (MTON)   33.43

5

8/21/1   COCA COLA CO (KO)   48.67

6

Technical Analysis/Reading Charts

Answers

8/21/1   MERCK & CO INC (MRK)   70.85

1

8/21/1   LILLY ELI & CO (LLY)   81.87

2

Mission Possible

Answers (cont.)

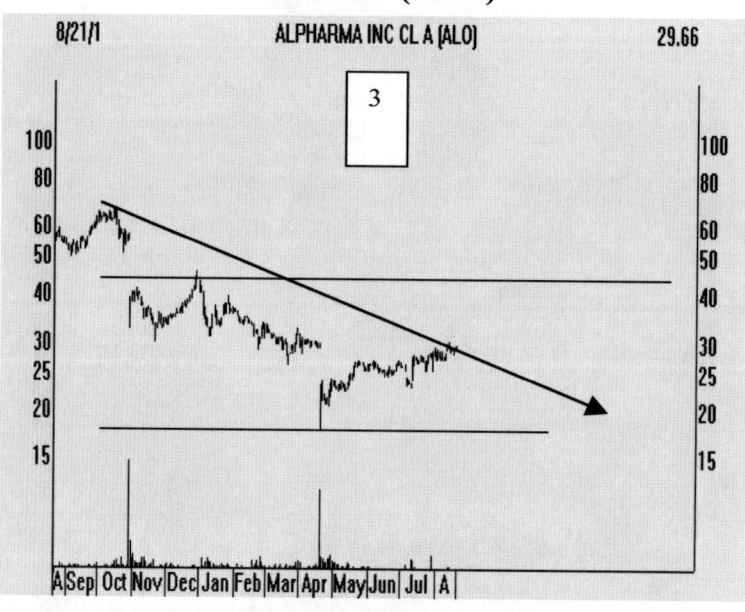

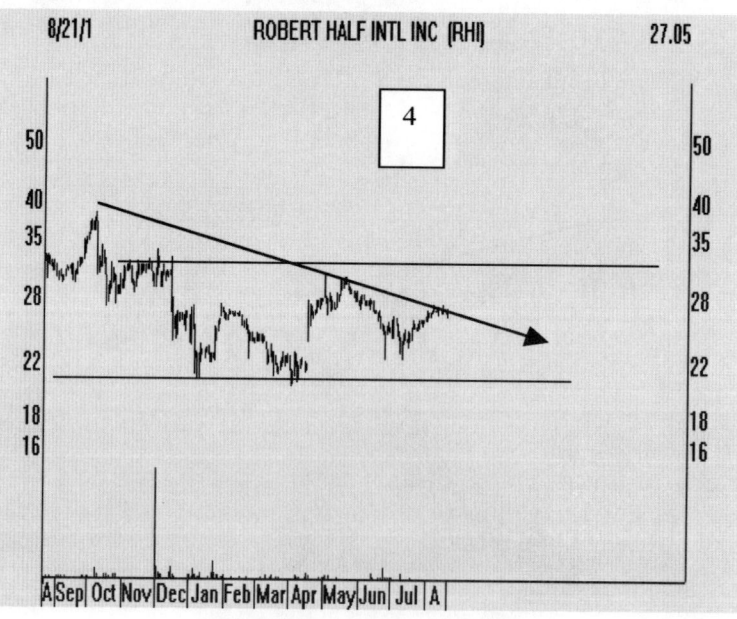

ALPHARMA INC CL A (ALO) — 8/21/1 — 29.66

3

ROBERT HALF INTL INC (RHI) — 8/21/1 — 27.05

4

Technical Analysis/Reading Charts

Answers (cont.)

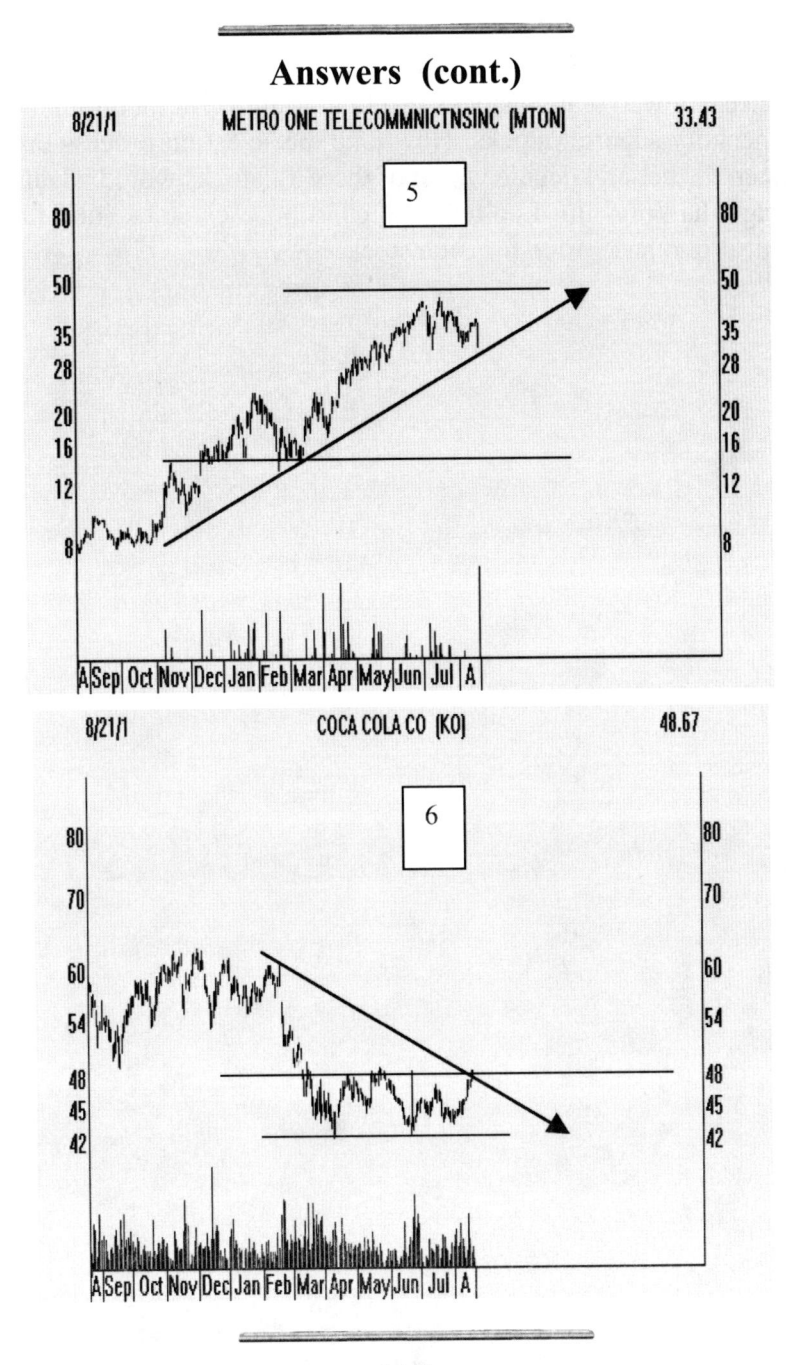

Mission Possible

In the previous chapter on fundamental analysis, the worksheet showed that 14 stocks meet our search criteria on fundamentally superior stocks. Now take the selection process one step further and decide which of these 14 stocks would advantage the portfolio. Looking at a chart on each stock, find the ideal purchase price for each stock.

Technical Analysis/Reading Charts

Chart Analysis

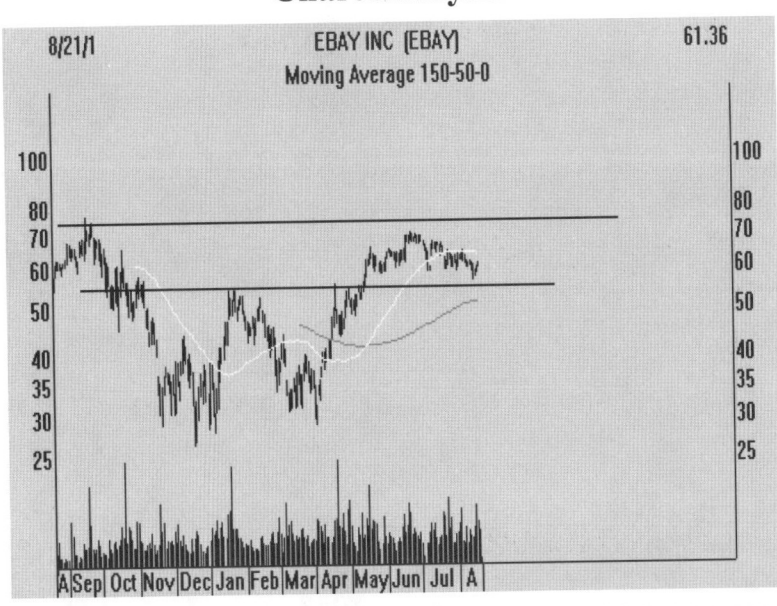

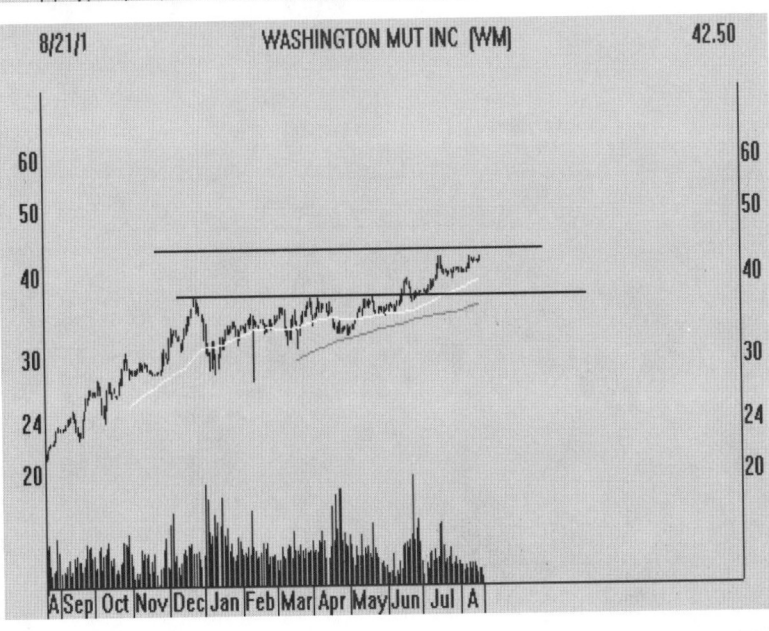

117

Mission Possible

Chart Analysis (cont.)

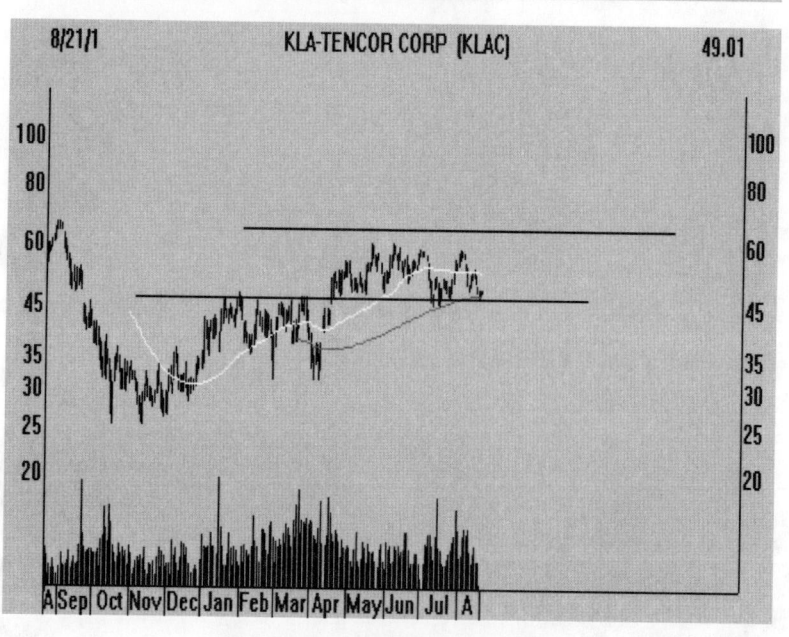

Technical Analysis/Reading Charts

Chart Analysis (cont.)

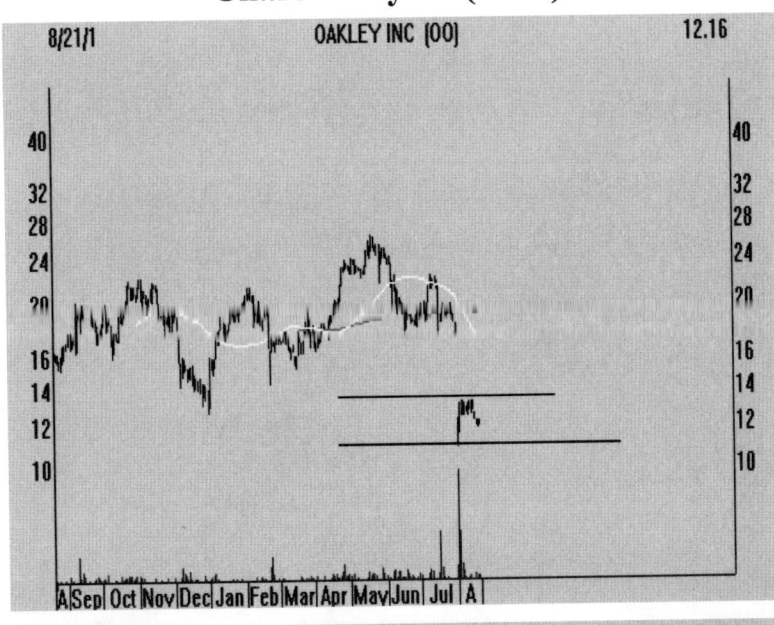

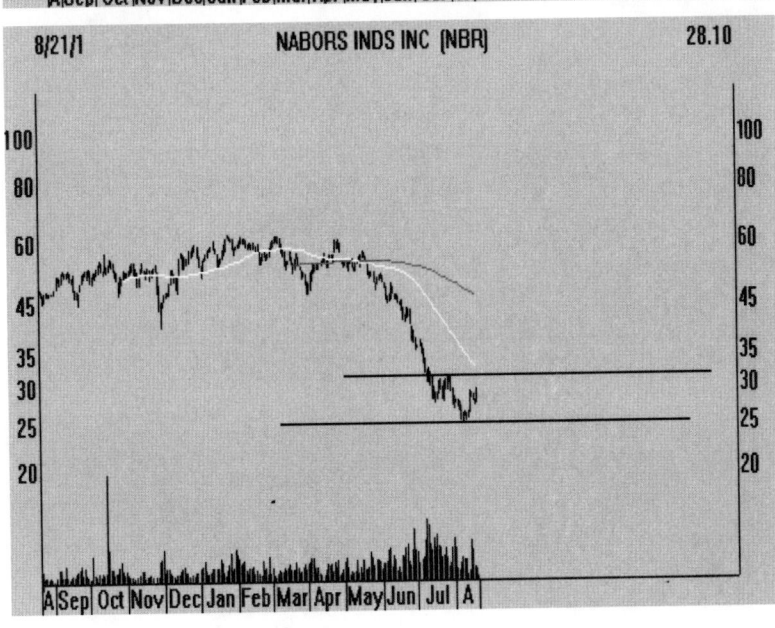

119

Chart Analysis (cont.)

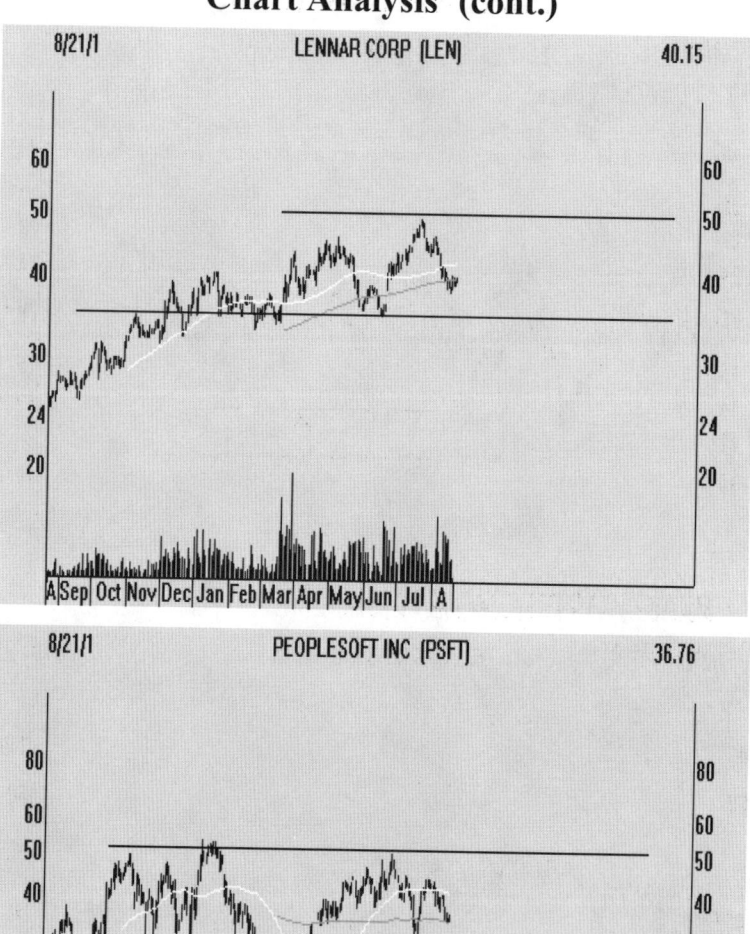

Technical Analysis/Reading Charts

Chart Analysis (cont.)

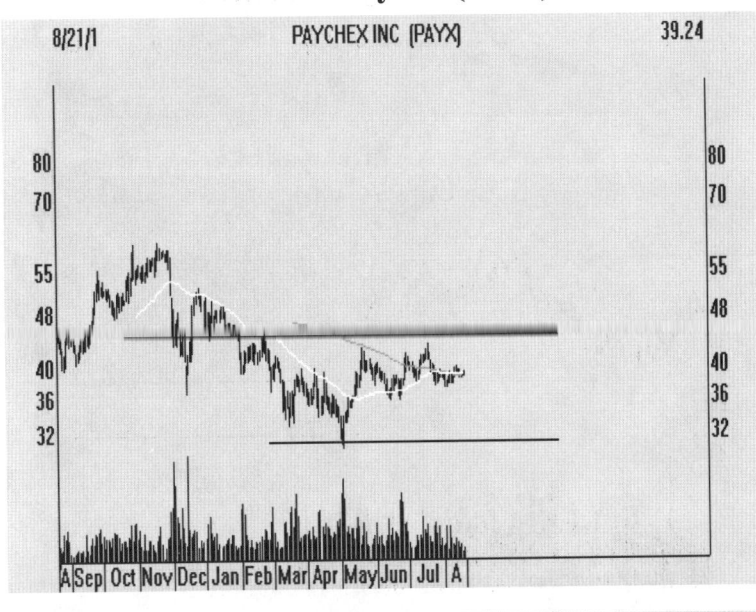

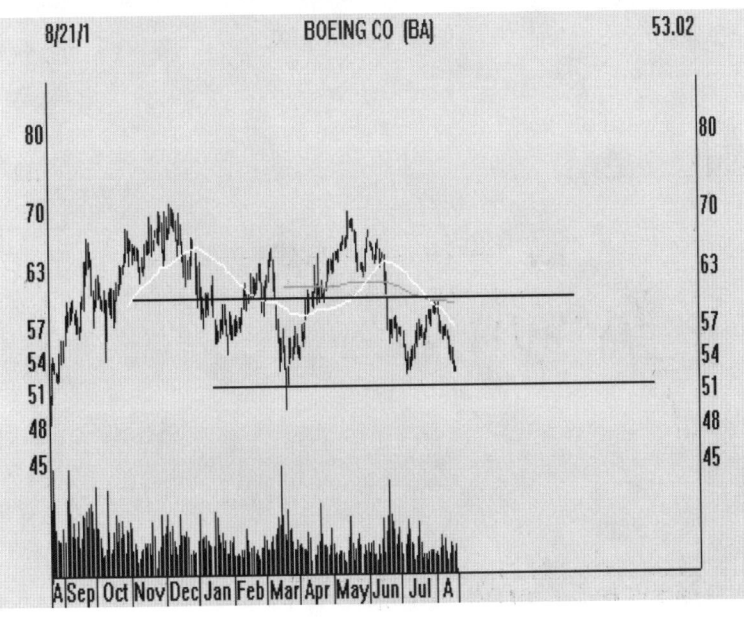

Mission Possible

Chart Analysis (cont.)

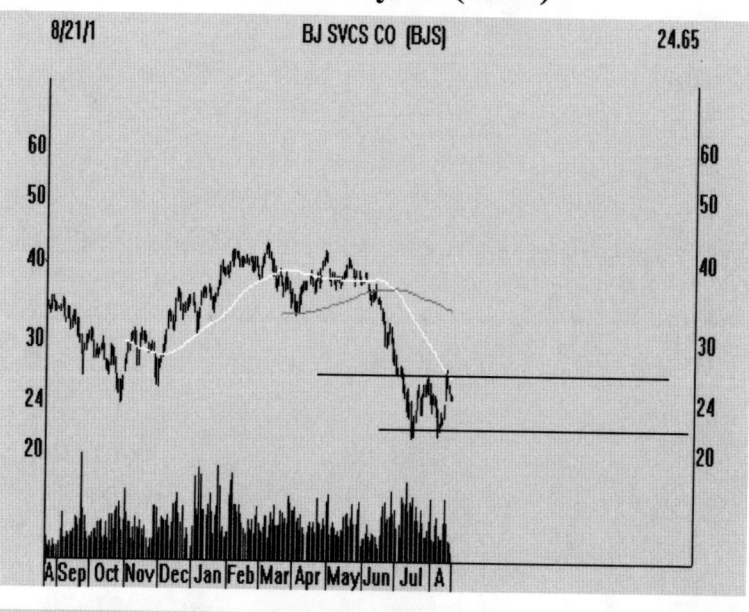

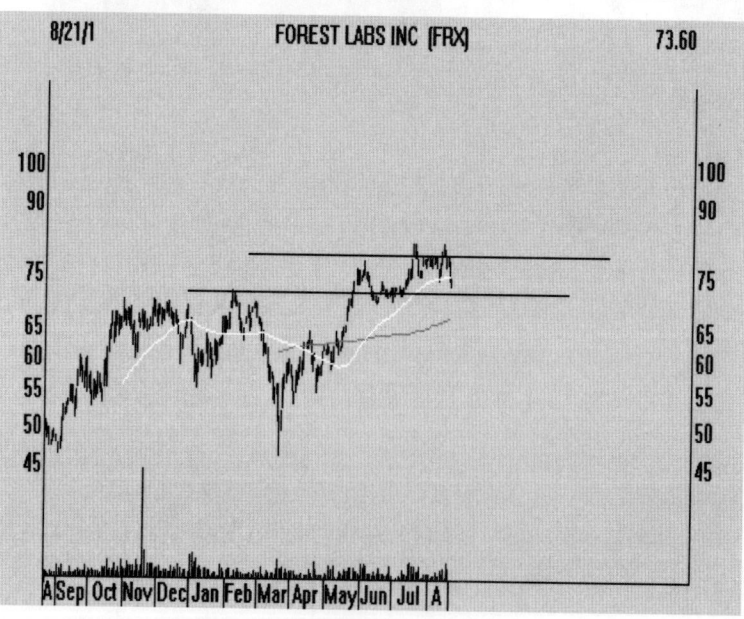

Technical Analysis/Reading Charts

Chart Analysis (cont.)

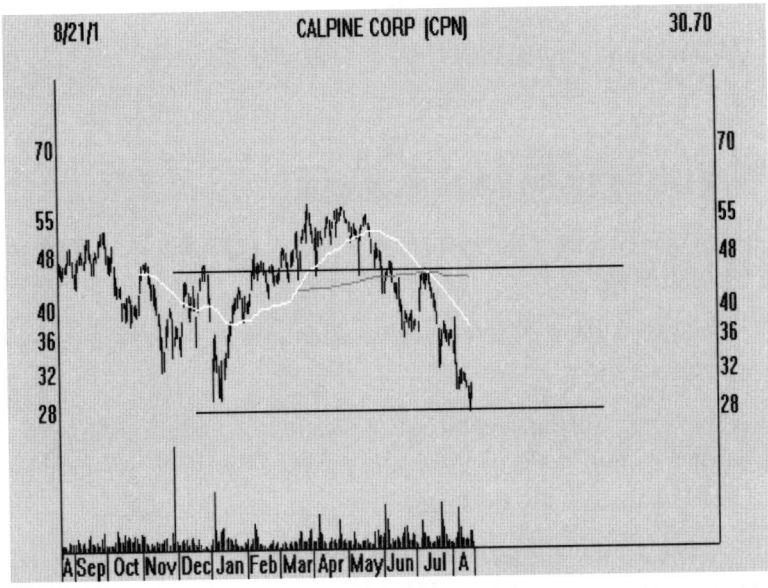

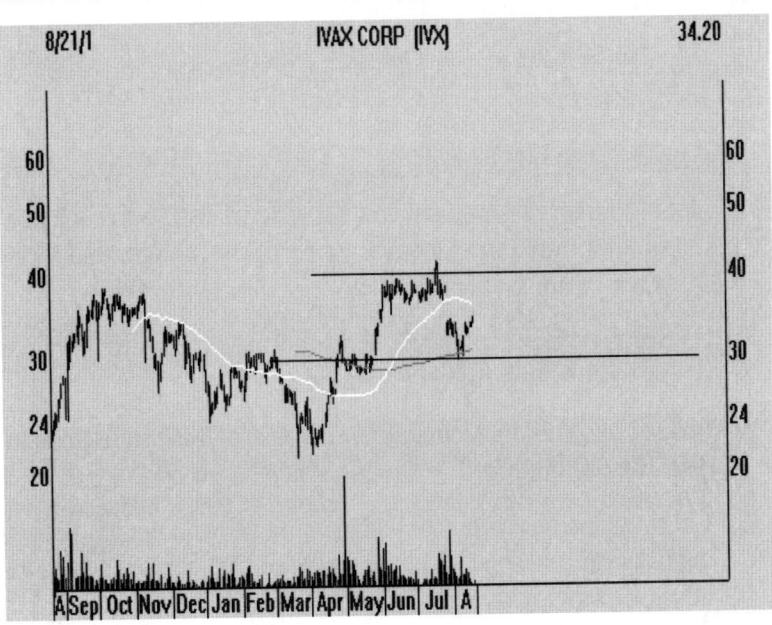

123

Mission Possible

1. Ebay fails the fundamental analysis selection process because the P/E ratio is more than four times the market.

2. Washington Mutual is a possible buy at 37½.

3. Global Marine fails the technical test because of its D accumulation/distribution ranking. Also, the price of the stock is below its 30-week moving average.

4. KLA-Tencor is a buy near 45, or if it breaks a new high on high volume.

5. Oakley's chart is so weak (breaking new lows) that the stock is not a buy.

6. Nabors fails our technical test because of its E accumulation/distribution ranking. Also, the price of the stock is below its 30-week moving average.

7. Lennar fails our technical test because of its D accumulation/distribution ranking.

8. PeopleSoft is a buy near 29.75, or if it breaks a new high on high volume.

9. PayChex is a buy near 33.

10. Boeing fails our technical test because of its E accumulation/distribution ranking. Also, the price of the stock is below its 30-week moving average.

11. BJ Services fails our technical test because the current price is below its 30-week moving average.

12. Forest Labs fails our technical test because of its D accumulation/distribution ranking.

13. Calpine fails our technical test because of its D accumulation/distribution ranking. Also, the price of the stock is below its 30-week moving average.

Technical Analysis/Reading Charts

14. IVAX would be a buy near 29½, or breaking a new high on high volume.

At the time of this writing, the stock market is currently in a bear market. If we would have been in a bull market, KLA-Tencor, PeopleSoft and PayChex would have failed our technical test, because all three stock's Relative Strength rankings are below 75. The only two stocks that would have passed the test in a Bull Market are Washington Mutual and IVAX. The use of the provided technical analysis worksheet will facilitate the selection of superior performing stocks.

Technical Analysis
Illustration 7

Company Name	Symbol	Stock Price	Accumulation/ Distribution Ranking (C or better)	Relative Strength Ranking (in bull market >75)	Resistance Level Price	Support Level Price	Moving Average 30-Week Price	Average Daily Volume	Ideal Buy Price
Ebay	EBAY	60.4	C	73	75	54.5	51	9.3	54.75
Wash Mut.	WM	38.4	B	90	43	37	35.8	4.1m	37.25
Global Marine	GLM	16.5	D	15	18.7	15	23.6	2.7m	15.25
KIA-Tencor	KLAC	49.8	B	65	67.4	44.8	47.6	7.6M	45 or NH
Oakley	OO	12.2	E	20	13.3	10.9	19	529K	N/B
Nabors	NBR	27.8	E	13	31.6	25	46.4	1.1M	N/B
Lenmar	LEN	46.5	D	76	49.8	34.8	39.9	932K	34.75 or N/H
PeopleSoft	PSFT	36	C	56	53/8	29.5	35.5	8M	29.75 or N/H
PayChex	PAYX	39.9	B	34	42.6	32.5	38.9	2.7M	33
BOEING	BA	53.8	E	36	59.5	49.3	59.3	3.3M	50
BJ Services	BJS	24.2	C	23	27.3	21.1	33.6	3.2M	21.5
Forest Labs	FRX	73.9	D	76	81.4	69.9	66.8	1M	70
Calpine	CPN	30	D	22	38.4	27.6	44.3	5.2M	N/B
Ivax	IVX	36.4	B	77	41.8	30.8	30.4	670K	29.5 or N/H

Mission Possible

Summary

1. Never buy a stock on a breakout that is not accompanied by a significant increase in volume. Look for a minimum of one and one-half times daily volume. The higher the volume, the better.

2. If the relative strength line is in a downward trend, do not buy the stock. Do not buy a stock that has broken out of its base if it is not trading above its 30-week moving average. Always draw trend lines and support and resistance lines, to create a visual picture of what the stock is doing. Once a stock has broken out above its resistance line, the stock usually will pull back close to the original resistance line to give the investor another chance to purchase the stock near the breakout price.

3. Purchase only stocks with an accumulation/distribution ranking of C or better, preferably ranked A or B.

4. In a bull market, purchase only stocks with a relative strength rank of 75 or higher. In a declining market, the relative strength ranking on many good growth stocks fall below the 75 relative strength ranking. Purchase a stock as close to the support line as possible.

9

When to Sell

All investors who try to build a portfolio will experience the sensation of having several stocks go down in price when the market still seems to be running strong. One question is always asked: When do you sell these losers?

The answer to this question is not easy. The first thing the CI should do is check the source for the stock's decline. Be sure that institutions are not selling the stock. Be sure the cause is not bad earnings. Stocks do not go down considerably without a reason. Each situation must be judged independently. If the situation looks to have a long-term effect on the stock, sell. Sometimes, you will not be able to determine the source for the selling pressure for a stock. On these types of situations where there is no apparent reason for the stock's decline, the best thing to do is sell. However, the road of investment blessings is paved with long-term holdings.

Many investors believe buying and selling is just part of investing in stocks. They watch the market hourly, believing they need to be buying something as the market goes up and selling as the market is moving down. Many books and computer programs offer assistance to the investor in timing the market. Not in the history of the market has anyone consistently been able to time the market. No computer program can do it yet. If there were such a program, the program would no longer work as soon as the public found out about it.

Market Efficiency and Taxes

The two best reasons for subscribing to the long-term investing theory is market efficiency and taxes. Buying and holding costs zero capital gains taxes until the gains are recognized. In other words, you do not pay taxes until you sell. Over the past decade or so, the stock market has gotten most of its gains in just a few days. If CIs missed those few days in the market, their portfolio would have suffered dearly. For example, in the 2,528 days of trading during the decade of the 1980s, an investment in the S&P 500 that missed the top 10 days of trading during the decade would have seen a drop in return from 17.5 percent to 12.6 percent annually. A top 20 days missed out of 2,528 and the return would have dropped to 9.3 percent. The top 40 days out of 2,528 days of trading would have only been less than 4 percent return. Think about it—40 days out of 2,528 days is just a mere 1.5 percent. So, missing the top 1.5 percent of the best days of trading during the 1980s annualized returns would have dropped from 17.5 percent to 3.9 percent. To put this a little clearer, a $10,000 investment earning 17.5 percent annually for 10 years would grow to $50,162. The same $10,000 investment earning 4 percent annually for 10 years would be worth a mere $14,802. Invest for the long term.

Homework has to be done by the CI, using technical analysis in each stock that is purchased. A slight drop in price is not a good reason to sell a stock. Stock investments are long-term commitments, so a slight drop in price should be of no concern. Most setbacks in fundamentally strong companies are just temporary setbacks. A bear market is just a temporary setback, because the average bear market lasts less than two years. A slight economic downturn, like a mild recession, is just temporary. What CIs must acknowledge is

When to Sell

that most investors are too emotional when it comes to investing in stocks. They vacillate, moved by every little wind that blows their way. CIs must be anchored and not be moved by every little swing in the market.

But there are occasions when selling your stock is timely. The best reason to sell a stock is when the fundamentals on the company start to break down. For instance, a company losing market share is a sign of serious problems. Another reason is when an industry group's fundamentals are starting to erode. For example, the long-distance telephone industry fundamentals have started to erode because of price slashing and the takeoff of cellular service. So the signs are there. Read them and act accordingly.

Selling Rules

Here are some selling rules every Christian investor should keep:

1. If the timeliness rankings of one of the companies you purchased drop below a 3 as published in Value Line, it is time to sell.

2. An EPS rank drop of more than 10 points is a possible sell signal. Revisit the fundamentals and technicals. If the company does not pass the screening rules mentioned in this book, consider selling the stock. But be wary. If a bear market rises, many companies' EPS rank will drop by at least 10 points, which is not necessarily a signal to sell on its own.

3. If a stock moves too fast, it will probably head down even quicker. A stock that is trading 50 percent higher than its 10-week moving average is a signal to possibly sell.

4. Two consecutive quarters of slower growth in earnings usually bodes bad news.

5. If a stock breaks below an upward trend line, it is a sell signal.

Mission Possible

6. If the accumulation distribution ranking drops below a C rating, as stated in Investors Business Daily, that is a possible sell signal.

7. If you buy a stock on a breakout and the breakout fails, sell the stock.

Use these rules so you will not fall into the trap of letting your emotions take control of your portfolio. If you are going to protect your capital, you must not fall in love with a stock. Highlight or write these rules down and apply them to every stock you purchase.

Other Things You Should Know

Do not pay attention to television personalities. Part of the technology meltdown of 2000 and 2001 was caused by television personalities pumping technology stocks. These pundits sell the sizzle that keeps investors glued to the television. Networks must sell commercial airtime to stay in business. If the networks cannot attract an audience, the advertisers will not pay the network to market their products. So, this is the reason there is so much sizzle on television, and the result was the dot com fever of 1998, 1999 and 2000.

1. *When the stock market is in a bear market, get out of the way and let the bear move on.* Do not purchase any new stocks in a down market until the market lets you know that a rally is in place. Know the health of the market. One way to do this is to study charts on the market indexes. No one can consistently predict the bottom. And again, you should not listen to the pundits' views—no matter how loved they are on Wall Street. Instead, keep a close eye on the Dow Jones 30, NASDAQ composite and the Standard & Poors 500. When you see a trend reversal, followed by heavy volume on the upside, this sign will often clue you in on a new market rally. Also, look for stocks shooting out of their bases with good earning surprises.

When to Sell

2. *Do not buy stocks, bonds or mutual funds on borrowed money (margin).* Purchasing an investment on margin is risky business, because it can turn sour in a short period of time. During adverse market conditions a portfolio on margin will show the investor how their profits, and often their capital, will diminish quickly. The problem I have witnessed with many investors is that when a portfolio is on margin and when a bear market shows its ugly head, the investors typically will ride the margin portfolio all the way down, hoping and believing the stocks would turn around until it is too late and most of their capital is lost. It is a bear that cannot be outrun. Proverbs 22:7 tells us, "The rich ruleth over the poor, and the borrower is servant to the lender." The Christian investor should be the lender and not the borrower. Stay away from the lure to use margin as a quick-fix to accumulate wealth.

3. *Prepare to shy away from options.* In this atmosphere, the wind of options whisper dangerously. Be steady. They are very risky. Options give you the choice of either buying or selling a stock at a designated price over a designated time period. Most options' contracts are short-termed. The right decision could be made on a stock, but if the timing is off by one day, all could be lost. Options are not investment vehicles for the long-term investor. Remember at all times just what you want, and expect your money to do for you. And especially do not day-trade. Day trading is not really investing—it is merely speculation on short-term moves in the market or stock. It sings the song of being very profitable; however, with taxes and the cost associated with trading the stocks, most individuals who try day trading fail to make a profit. Compared to the usual small profit, the risk associated with day trading is extremely high.

4. *Penny stocks are a plague to avoid.* Most people think of penny stocks as stocks that trade below one dollar and trade in cents; however, by almost literal definition, penny stocks trade for $5 per share or less. It has been my experience that CIs should shy away from stocks that trade less than $10 per share. Usually, when

a stock trades for less than $10 per share, there is something wrong with the stock. Most profitable companies will trade above $10 per share. When doing your search criteria for fundamentally superior stocks, keep your selection process to stocks that trade above $10 per share.

5. *Do not take advice from a biased adviser.* There are many conflicts of interest in this world, but the most damaging kind occurs when the conflict is obviously stacked against you. A biased adviser is often a commissioned adviser. These types of advisers get paid when you move money. If true long-term investing were practiced by the clients, biased advisers would have to get another job. Many of these biased advisers never learn the strategies that are written in this book. These advisers do not get paid for their stock-picking savvy or for developing a winning portfolio. They get paid for selling a nontangible product (stocks, bonds and mutual funds), and they are well compensated for what they do. Many of these advisers will not take the time or effort to learn the fundamentals for selecting superior performing stocks. But many will put in the time and effort to learn to be better salesmen. What the CI needs is not a good seller, but a good unbiased adviser.

6. *Be aware of the credibility problems with brokerage firms that offer investment banking and independent analyst advice.* A firm that offers both has a conflict of interest with the consumer. These firms claim to have a "Chinese wall" between the various divisions of a financial firm. However, it is almost impossible for this Chinese wall to exist. They supposedly work on the idea that there is a wall where the investment banking side of the firm does not share information with the analyst and the retail brokerage side of the firm.

When a brokerage firm's investment banking division is pending new shares of a corporation, or raising new capital for a bond issue for the corporation, most of the time the analysts are not able to use their independent judgment as to the desirability of that corporation seeking investment banking business. For example, suppose that XYZ company needed to raise $4 billion to build a few new plants

When to Sell

for the company to compete in its industry. This $4 billion deal will make the investment banking department millions of dollars for the brokerage firm. It challenges credibility to an absurd extreme to believe in the independence of the analyst giving advice to the public about XYZ company. If the analyst said that the company is a "sell," the executives for XYZ will move their investment banking business to another firm that will not recommend its company as a sell. So, if the analyst tells the truth, the brokerage firm loses millions of dollars.

Lose millions of dollars? No sir, these firms do not want to lose millions of dollars. This is one reason you hardly ever hear of a sell in the brokerage and analyst community. They typically rank stocks as a buy—accumulate or hold. So, there is a problem with honesty in the advice of an analyst who works with a brokerage firm that offers investment banking services. And nearly all your large retail brokerage companies offer both investment banking and analyst services. Another reason to learn to analyze and research your own investments.

7. *Do not average down when purchasing a stock.* If you buy a stock at $36 a share and if it drops to $26 a share, do not average down by purchasing additional shares. Many advisers talk investors into purchasing additional shares of a stock that dropped in price by saying, "If you liked it at $36, you should love it at $26." This is faulty thinking. After doing your homework and the stock looks fundamentally strong, do your technical homework and buy near the support line. If you did your homework and purchased at the correct price, you should never average down because if the stock goes below the support line, the stock will usually drop a considerable amount. When this happens, the relative strength line will drop and more than likely the accumulation/distribution ranking will drop. Buying a stock when it falls below support is against everything you have learned.

Mission Possible

8. *Do not enter a stop-loss order.* Stop-loss order is when you place an order with a brokerage company to sell your stock when it drops to a certain price. For example, let's say you purchased Home Depot at $50 and you decided you did not want to lose more than 10 percent of your investment on the stock. A 10 percent loss would make you sell the stock at $45. An investor with this mentality could then turn around after he purchased the stock at $50 and enter a stop-loss order at $45. This would tell the specialist on the floor of the New York Stock Exchange to stop what he is doing and sell your stock at $45 if the stock tends to trade down to that price in the future. The specialist will not sell your stock unless the stock drops to $45, leaving you with unlimited upside potential and limited downside risk. This sounds good, but the problem is that this works good in theory, but it does not work in reality.

I have seen the specialist run a stock down to get the person out of stop-loss order, then turn around and run the stock right back up to the original trading price. This type of transaction is not supposed to happen, but it does. I once had 500 shares of Office Depot that I had entered a stop-loss order at $23 per share. The stock was trading in the $26 to $27 range. The specialist ran the stock down to $23, which was the lowest price for the day, and sold my shares. Office Depot closed at $27 for the day. If I would have not entered the stop-loss order, I would not have been whipsawed out of the stock.

If you have a place where you would like to limit the potential loss on a stock, keep the price in your mind and watch the stock closely. If the stock price drops to a place where the investor need to limit loss, enter a market order to sell out of your position. If the CI is in need of funds and is forced to sell a stock to gather some cash, always sell your losers first. Never sell your stock winners first. Let your winners run and trim the losers. Also, when purchasing and selling investments, be careful not to overstress tax advantages, and purchase otherwise poor investments as a result. The CI should prefer capital gains to dividends.

When to Sell

Stay Positive

The Christian's outlook of the future must always stay positive. An old stockbroker once told me, "I have never met a man who had accumulated wealth that was not optimistic." This old man was an unbeliever, but his observation was correct. The Bible tells us that even those who believe and trust in Christ will suffer temptation. By His strength, we can come out of all trials victorious. We may end up with several battle wounds, but we win the war.

Knowing the outcome as being positive should give each Christian an optimistic outlook for the future. Like the old song says, "The God that has never lost a battle stands by me."

Do not allow doom and gloom to enter your heart or spirit. "We are more than conquerors through him that loved us" (Romans 8:37). A pessimistic outlook engenders failure in business and jeopardizes your walk with Christ Jesus. In the stock market, pessimists are called bears, optimists are called bulls. In the long run, bears are always the losers. God has called us to be winners, not losers.

Do not be shaken if you make a mistake. We all do. It is not the end of the world to purchase stock at the wrong time. In the early stages of trying to learn these strategies, you will have to learn from your errors. The more you study and learn, the less you will go astray. Flaws in your decision making and wrong turns will lessen in time. Believe it. When sinners first give their hearts to Jesus, they tend to make more mistakes than the seasoned Christian who has been living for the Lord for years.

We must remember, "We have an advocate with the Father" (1 John 2:1). His name is Jesus Christ. If we stumble along life's path, we ask Jesus to forgive us of our sin, and He will. If we fail to ask Jesus to forgive us when we sin, the sin will grow into a "root of bitterness" (Hebrews 12:15) that will damn our souls. Likewise, when the CI makes a mistake investing hard-earned money, losses must be cut quickly. Otherwise, hardship and the possibility of death to our financial well-being will occur. As we become more sanctified with Christ, the fewer mistakes we will make in our walk. Likewise, the more we study these investment strategies and put them to use, the less investment mistakes we will make. It is an issue of knowledge in faith and faith in knowledge.

10

Do Not Lose Focus

In working through the past chapters on accumulating wealth, you should have discovered the truth of God's Word—that He has given us the power to obtain wealth. If you study the techniques in this book and learn to apply them along with God's Word, He will establish you on the road of accumulated wealth. Accumulating wealth can become a reality.

Promise yourself that you will start saving and investing a portion of your income. Follow the fundamental and technical guidelines in this book. Never buy a stock on a rumor; always remember to do your homework. If you find a company you like, but the company does not meet your search criteria, do not buy the stock. Never deviate from your investment plan. Remember, even in bad times—and bad times will surely come—you are on the road to established wealth. Now that you have a game plan, do not underestimate its importance. If you follow the guidelines in this book in a disciplined manner, you will be on the narrow road that leads to accumulated wealth. Finally, vow to be consistent to your investment plan. Do not make any exceptions.

Sometimes we Christians get to a point where we ask ourselves,

Mission Possible

"What am I doing? Where am I going? Are You still there, God?" We come to the realization that we have lost focus of what God has called us to do. It is nice to accumulate wealth; however, our main purpose in life is to adhere to God's calling. Each Christian has a calling on his or her life. It may not be to stand in a pulpit and preach, or even to teach a Sunday school class. Your calling may be just to witness to your friends and neighbors about the good things of God. Whatever your calling, do not lose focus. Most true believers in Jesus Christ will know in their heart what Christ has called them to do. Many new converts are unaware of their calling, but time will usually tell them what God has called them to do for the kingdom of God. We were not called here just to fill up space and get rich. However, God did call us to win over the lost, and that is our great commission.

Personal Mission Statement

Life today is so complicated and fast-paced. Every minute of each day is spoken for. Many times we lose sight of our calling because we are engulfed with things we are trying to accomplish. The important things seem to vanish before our eyes. In my personal life, it seems that at times my wheels were spinning, but I was not going anywhere. In these situations I go back and pull out the personal mission statement I wrote for my business and my personal life. Because it is easy for me to lose sight of what is important, my personal mission statement helps keep me focused. My mission is to teach, encourage and inspire others toward faithful stewardship in all God has given them. We must stay focused on God's calling in our lives and not the things of the world. Colossians 3:2 says, "Set your affection on things above, not on things on the earth." Stay focused on God; accumulating wealth is a dividend for serving God. The blessings of God are just by-products of a personal relationship with Jesus Christ. Proverbs 28:20 tells us, "A faithful man shall abound with blessings." The man who is faithful to God's calling will follow God's commandments and be blessed.

We should not focus on the blessings, but on God because He is the source of all blessings. Take the time to write your own personal mission statement. Look at it, read it and memorize it. Stay focused on your mission in life.

The Mission Is Possible

God has a designated time and season for all things. In the process of accumulating wealth, some Christians want it yesterday. But it takes a while to get to the status of life we desire. The Bible tells us, "Cast thy bread upon the waters: for thou shalt find it after many days" (Ecclesiastes 11:1).

Sometimes God's promises toward us do not come in the allotted time we desire to receive them. However, God is never late; He is always on time. Ecclesiastes 3:17 tells us, "There is a time there for every purpose and for every work."

God has an allotted timetable for all things. We are not to get anxious but wait on the Lord. If we meet God's conditions mentioned in this book, God does give us power to accumulate wealth. Because we know that if God promised something in His Word, it will come to fruition. Second Corinthians 1:20 tells us, "For all the promises of God in him are yea, and in him Amen, unto the glory of God by us."

God is telling us that all His promises toward us are yes and let it be so. God's promises to us are always truthful; not one of God's promises to the believer is NO. We just must meet the conditions. The mission is possible!

Appendix

Worksheet 1
Questionnaire

1. What primary goal do you have in mind for your portfolio? Please check one.

    A. _____ Retirement
    B. _____ Education
    C. _____ Home Purchase
    D. _____ Leave an Estate

2. What is the time frame you have in mind for meeting your primary goal as indicated in question 1? Please check one.

    A. _____ 1 to 3 years
    B. _____ 3 to 5 years
    C. _____ 5 to 10 years
    D. _____ over 10 years

3. Please indicate your investment objectives for your portfolio by checking one of the boxes below.

    A. _____ Income and Growth
    B. _____ Conservative Low Risk Growth
    C. _____ Moderate Risk Growth
    D. _____ Aggressive Growth

Mission Possible

Lower levels of risk are generally associated with income-producing investments, while higher levels of risk are generally associated with growth-oriented investments. Please keep in mind when responding to question #4.

Please note that your portfolio should be managed to seek total returns through the combination of capital appreciation and dividend income.

4. Generally, higher return expectations have higher levels of risk (including variability of returns and risk of loss) associated with these expectations. Lower return expectations are generally associated with lower levels of risk and volatility. Please indicate by checking one box below your return/risk expectation for your portfolio.

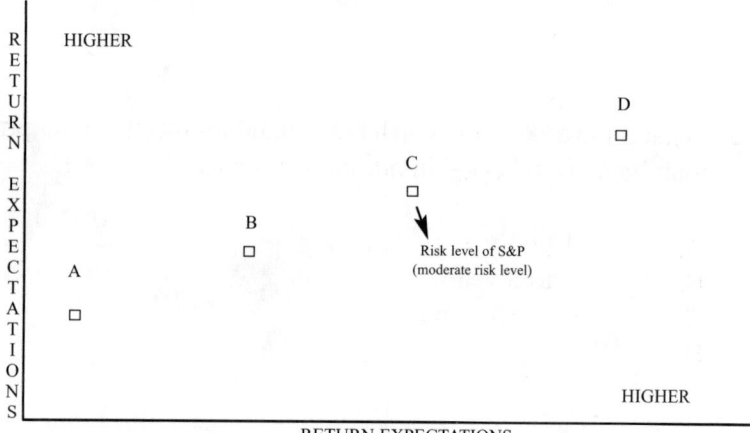

RETURN EXPECTATIONS (y-axis, HIGHER at top) vs RETURN EXPECTATIONS (x-axis, HIGHER at right)

- A □ (low return, low risk)
- B □
- C □ ← Risk level of S&P (moderate risk level)
- D □ (high return, high risk)

5. Sometimes Christians should use a global investment strategy looking for a combination of foreign and domestic investments. In fact, many mutual funds that invest predominantly in domestic securities may hold a certain amount of foreign securities. Foreign investing provides the potential for higher investment returns, but also has certain associated risks, such

Appendix

as market and currency risks. Please indicate the level of foreign securities holdings you would prefer.

 A. _____ Zero foreign holdings
 B. _____ Low level of foreign holdings
 C. _____ Moderate level of foreign holdings
 D. _____ High level of foreign holdings

6. Check the one statement that best describes your attitude toward investment risk.

 A. _____ Strongly dislike risk—I consider preservation of capital more important than investment return.
 B. _____ Desires little risk—Preservation of capital is important; however, growth is also important.
 C. _____ Desires moderate risk—I am willing to risk some capital for the potential of an above-the-ordinary gain.
 D. _____ Risk taker—I am willing to risk a substantial portion of assets invested if there is a chance of doubling or tripling the value of capital.

7. Please check the one statement that indicates your response to the following: I am comfortable with investments that may go down in value from time to time, if they offer the potential for higher returns.

 A. _____ Disagree
 B. _____ Somewhat agree
 C. _____ Agree
 D. _____ Strongly agree

8. Once you begin taking withdrawals from your portfolio, how long will the money in the account have to last before it is depleted?

Mission Possible

    A. _____   Less than 1 year
    B. _____   1-5 years
    C. _____   6-10 years
    D. _____   11 or more years

9. Please check the statement that best approximates the amount of CURRENT income your investments will need to generate as an annual percentage of your total income from all sources.

    A. _____   31% - 50%
    B. _____   16% - 30%
    C. _____   6% - 15%
    D. _____   0% - 5%

10. How long could you cover monthly living expenses with cash and investments you currently have on hand?

    A. _____   Up to 3 months
    B. _____   3-6 months
    C. _____   6-12 months
    D. _____   12 months or more

11. What is your outlook for your future income from sources other than investments?

    A. _____   It will greatly decrease.
    B. _____   It will stay the same.
    C. _____   It will increase, but not by much.
    D. _____   It will greatly increase.

For each question that you answered:
Answer A gives you 0 points.   Answer B gives you 5 points.
Answer C gives you 10 points.   Answer D gives you 15 points.
Question #1 is the only question not scored.

Total score of 0 to 50 is a conservative risk portfolio.
Total score of 51 to 110 is a moderate risk portfolio.
Total score of 111 to 150 is an aggressive risk portfolio.

Appendix

Worksheet 2
Stock Mutual Fund Buyer's Worksheet

Fund Name	Fund Category	Quote Symbol	Sharpe Ratio (Higher is better.)	Beta	Total Assets (SM) (Lower is better.)	Manager in place since (Year)	Manager's Name	Annual Operating Expense Ratio (Lower is better.)	Total Returns Avg. 5yr.	Annualized 3yr.	Total Return 1yr.

Mission Possible

Worksheet 3
Bond Mutual Fund Buyer's Worksheet

Fund Name	Fund Category	Quote Symbol	Sharpe Ratio (Higher is better.)	Avg. Credit Quality	Total Assets (SM) (Lower is better.)	Manager in place since (Year)	Manager's Name	Annual Operating Expense Ratio (Lower is better.)	Total Returns Avg. 5yr.	Annualized 3yr.	Total Return 1yr.

Appendix

Worksheet 4

Budget Worksheet

Gross Income Per Month .... _____
    Minus Federal Tax .... _____
    Minus FICA .... _____
    Minus Medicare .... _____
    Minus State Tax .... _____
    Minus Local Tax .... _____
    Minus Retirement Plan Contributions
        (401K, 403-B, etc.) .... _____
    Minus Health Insurance .... _____
    Minus Life Insurance .... _____
    Minus Flexible Spending Account
        (Medical) .... _____
    Minus Flexible Spending Account
        (Dependent Care) .... _____
    Minus Garnishments .... _____

        Total Net Income .... _____

Expenses

Charitable Donations
    Tithes .... _____
    Offerings .... _____
    Missions .... _____
    Other .... _____
        Total Charitable Donations .... _____
        Budget Guide .... _____
        Difference .... _____

Mission Possible

Automobile

Car Payment/Lease	_____
Gasoline and Oil	_____
Maintenance	_____
Parts	_____
Insurance	_____
Taxes	_____
Total Automobile Expense	_____
Budget Guide	_____
Difference	_____

Housing

Mortgage/Rent	_____
Second Mortgage	_____
Insurance	_____
Taxes	_____
Maintenance	_____
Furnishing	_____
Yard Service	_____
Other	_____
Total Housing Expense	_____
Budget Guide	_____
Difference	_____

Food

Groceries	_____
Dining Out	_____
Total Food Expense	_____
Budget Guide	_____
Difference	_____

Recurring Bills

Electricity	_____
Natural Gas	_____

Appendix

Telephone .... _____
Water and Sewage .... _____
Sanitation .... _____
Other .... _____
    Total Recurring Bills .... _____
        Budget Guide .... _____
        Difference .... _____

Insurance (omit if paid pretax through company)

Life .... _____
Medical .... _____
Disability .... _____
Long-term Care .... _____
Other .... _____
    Total Insurance Expense ...... _____
        Budget Guide .... _____
        Difference .... _____

Debts

Credit Cards .... _____
Loans and Notes .... _____
Bank Charges .... _____
Other .... _____
    Total Debts Expense .... _____
        Budget Guide .... _____
        Difference .... _____

Recreation and Entertainment

Activities and Trips .... _____
Vacation .... _____
Health Club .... _____
Social Club .... _____
Other .... _____
    Total Recreation and
        Entertainment Expense ..... _____

Mission Possible

Budget Guide . . . . _____
Difference . . . . _____

Leisure

Books and Magazines . . . . _____
Cable . . . . _____
Sporting Goods . . . . _____
Toys and Games . . . . _____
Internet Expense . . . . _____
Total Leisure Expense . . . . _____
Budget Guide . . . . _____
Difference . . . . _____

Clothing

Total Clothing Expense . . . . _____
Budget Guide . . . . _____
Difference . . . . _____

Child Care

Day Care . . . . _____
Baby-sitter . . . . _____
School Tuition . . . . _____
Materials . . . . _____
School Transportation . . . . _____
Children's Club . . . . _____
Total Child Care Expense . . . . . _____
Budget Guide . . . . _____
Difference . . . . _____

Savings and Investments

Total Savings and Investments . _____
Budget Guide . . . . _____
Difference . . . . _____

Appendix

Health Care
- Dental .... _____
- Hospital .... _____
- Physician .... _____
- Drugs .... _____
- Other .... _____
    - Total Health Care Expense .... _____
    - Budget Guide .... _____
    - Difference .... _____

Miscellaneous
- Photos .... _____
- Pet Care .... _____
- Advertising .... _____
- Beauty Supplies .... _____
- Haircuts .... _____
- Personal Care .... _____
- Gifts .... _____
- Laundry .... _____
- Cash .... _____
- All Other Expenses Not Mentioned .. _____
    - Total Miscellaneous Expense .. _____
    - Budget Guide .... _____
    - Difference .... _____

TOTAL OF ALL EXPENSES _____
- Net Income .... _____
- Less Expenses .... _____
- Balance .... _____
- Difference .... _____

Mission Possible

Worksheet 5
Fundamental Analysis Worksheet

Company Name	Stock Symbol	Stock Price	P/E Ratio	Debt to Equity Ratio	EPS Rank >80	Min. Annual EPS growth >20%	Min. prior Qtr. EPS growth >25%	Min. projected next year EPS growth >30%

Appendix

Technical Analysis Worksheet 6

Company Name	Symbol	Stock Price	Accumulation/ Distribution Ranking (C or better)	Relative Strength Ranking (in bull market >75)	Resistance Level Price	Support Level Price	Moving Average 30-Week Price	Average Daily Volume	Ideal Buy Price